Dharma in America

America now is home to approximately five million Hindus and Jains. Their contribution to the economic and intellectual growth of the country is unquestionable. *Dharma in America* aims to explore the role of Hindu and Jain Americans in diverse fields such as:

- education and civic engagements
- medicine and healthcare
- music.

Providing a concise history of Hindus and Jains in the Americas over the last two centuries, *Dharma in America* also gives some insights into the ongoing issues and challenges these important ethnic and religious groups face in America today.

Pankaj Jain is Associate Professor of Philosophy and Religion at the University of North Texas, USA.

Dharma in America

A Short History of Hindu-Jain Diaspora

Pankaj Jain

LONDON AND NEW YORK

First published 2020
by Routledge
2 Park Square, Milton Park, Abingdon, Oxon OX14 4RN

and by Routledge
52 Vanderbilt Avenue, New York, NY 10017

Routledge is an imprint of the Taylor & Francis Group, an informa business

British Library Cataloguing-in-Publication Data
A catalogue record for this book is available from the British Library

Library of Congress Cataloging-in-Publication Data
A catalog record has been requested for this book

ISBN: 978-1-138-56544-9 (hbk)
ISBN: 978-1-138-56545-6 (pbk)
ISBN: 978-1-315-12302-8 (ebk)

Typeset in Times New Roman
by Taylor & Francis Books

Contents

Preface

Being Hindu, being Jain, being American

I was born in a small town called Pali in the Indian state of Rajasthan. This town has a long history of Jains and Hindu living together. As early as 912 CE, a magnificent Jain temple was built in the heart of this town. Also in the heart of the town, a replica of Gujarat's famous Somnath Temple was constructed by the great King Kumarpal in 1152 CE. This Hindu ruler adopted and patronized Jainism in his late years. Growing up in Pali from the early 1970s to late 1980s, I experienced and observed both Hinduism and Jainism at first hand. My mother remains a devotee of the Hindu god Hanuman, and my father practices Jainism. My grandmother (my father's mother), who always lived with us, used to walk daily to the couple of Jain temples that were about 2 kilometers from our home, before she would take her first sip of water and breakfast. She would perform all her rituals at the temples for a couple of hours, walk back to our home, recite her Jain verses, and then start her day. In addition to the Jainism practiced by my grandmother, I observed and often participated with all my Hindu friends in visiting our local Hindu temple in the evenings, mostly to enjoy the sweets that the priest would distribute. We also celebrated several Indian festivals and holidays, such as Diwali and Holi with fun and frolic. My parents also took us to see historical and religious towns in the western Indian states of Rajasthan and Gujarat and the southern Indian states of Karnataka and Tamilnadu that has several Hindu and Jain temples. Almost all of my early life I learned, observed, and experienced the theologies, geographies, and histories of Hinduism and Jainism.

However, like most other middle-class kids, religion was never the center of my life as a young boy. My father was the first-generation college graduate from an Engineering College in the southern state of Karnataka, and I was expected to follow in his footsteps. Since my grandmother did not allow him to study abroad, I was the next bearer of that dream in our family. As soon as I completed my Computer Science degree, I took the GRE and TOEFL to come to the United States. When my student visa application was rejected twice, I worked as a software engineer for a few years and finally could come to New Jersey in 1996 on the H1B visa. Since the 1990s, thousands of Indian engineers have taken this route each year to go to the United States, and the trend continues today.

As I was about to leave India, I started realizing the importance of my Indian heritage and culture, something that had been just a footnote for me until then. Our employer invited two American software experts to India to teach us a programming language called Smalltalk. As the training came to an end, our Human Resources department gifted them a copy of the *Bhagavad Gī tā* and a few albums of Indian classical music. This gifting activity was my first wake-up alarm. These gems of Indian culture that my colleagues valued enough to gift to foreign guests remained far from my thoughts and perhaps from millions of other young Indians whose first and foremost goal remains to become employable, mostly in STEM (Science, Technology, Engineering, and Mathematics) related fields. As I was about to lose and leave my motherland for a foreign country, I started my journey to learn about its culture and heritage. I started visiting the local Ramakrishna Vedanta Center in Hyderabad and studied several books on Indian philosophy, spirituality, and history. I also started practicing yoga and meditation and started listening to Indian classical music, all for the first time, in my last year of being in India. After few years of arriving and living in New Jersey, this journey to study Indian culture took the significant next step when I left my IT career and became a full-time MA student in the Department of Religion at Columbia University and later a PhD student in the Department of Religious Studies at the University of Iowa. After completing my PhD and teaching for a couple of years at Rutgers and North Carolina State Universities, I moved to the Dallas area which is where I continue to imagine being a Jain, being a Hindu, *and* being an American.

As I continue to live "the American dream" in these last more than two decades, I have observed and worked with hundreds of other Hindus and Jains in North America. Some of them, hopefully, will be able to resonate with the information presented in this book. Many academic and popular books trace the history of Hinduism in America. Almost all these books focus on temples and organizations that are about practicing Hinduism in one way or the others, such as Hindu-inspired meditation movements or practicing yoga. However, for most Hindus and Jains in America, and in India, life is not just about practicing spirituality. For many Hindus and Jains, food and healthcare practices, music, and the education system in America continue to remind them to keep their ancient traditions alive in their new adopted land where they are a tiny minority. This book is a humble compilation and recollection of some such Hindu and Jain American attempts in the last few centuries in the Americas.

Acknowledgments

I am now taking this opportunity to acknowledge all the people who have helped me in this journey. I have profound gratitude for the Faculty Development Leave and Scholarly and Creative Activity Award in 2018 from the University of North Texas that helped me travel and undertake research for the book. Thanks are also due to the anonymous reviewers who significantly improved the manuscript with their detailed comments. I am grateful to colleagues, such as Vivek Virani, Lisa Owen, Balwant Dixit, and Dan Neuman for valuable inputs.

I thank several Jain Americans, who have helped me with their useful insights, such as Anant Jain, Manoj Jain, Sulekh Jain, Udai Jain, Shefali Jhaveri, Lalit Kothari, Bhuvanendra Kumar, Nikin Mehta, Pravin Mehta, Shreyas Mehta, Tansukh Salgia, Dilip Shah, Jitubhai Shah, Pravin Shah, and Pradeep Vaidya, and other Jains in North America.

I thank Ayurvedic experts and practitioners, such as Vasant Lad, Dhanada Kulkarni, and Amba Prabhakar. I thank Manoj Govindraj, Sanjeev Ramabhadran, and other Indian classical music experts for their musical insights. I thank my friends in the Dallas area who provided valuable comments for the chapter on civic engagement. Of course, any omission or error in the book remains my own.

I thank my parents, my wife, and our two kids, who continue to endure my long absences, physical and mental, for research and writing, and who keep me grounded as my fellow Hindu-Jain Americans. Finally, please visit Facebook.com/HinduJainDiaspora for the relevant images and information related to different chapters of the book.

1 Introduction

On a bright spring morning in 2015, when I was co-hosting a Study Abroad Fair at my university, the University of North Texas, my colleague and I were hoping to sign up students to take them to India in the summer. As a couple of curious students stopped by, we asked them if they would like to go to India, the largest democracy in the world. Although students did not seem too excited to make any comparison between the two democracies of India and the USA, I began wondering if there could be any other connections between the two nations, seemingly poles apart. One of them is the hallmark of the "Eastern" world and the other is that of the "Western" world. As Nico Slate (2019) put it, these are the two most prominent and most diverse democracies, yet to fulfill their dreams of making freedom and democracy genuinely available to all their marginalized and minority communities.

As is widely known, the term "Indian" is already used to refer to the Native Americans living across North America. Perhaps because of this reason, a recent book about Indian Americans was entitled "The Other Indians" (Lal 2008). Following the "other" pronoun, there is another book about Indian Americans that referred to Indian Americas as "the other one percent" (Chakravorty et al. 2017). The population of Indian Americans in America is now a little over 1 percent of the total American population. However, this 1 percent is differentiated from the wealthiest 1 percent of Americans that "owns more of the country's wealth than at any time in the past 50 years" (Ingraham 2017).

Apart from the way those other authors have tried to write about Indian Americans, can there be some other way to see the connections between India and the USA? Similarly, Indian Americans know that they are a complete digit of 1 percent and no more a footnote in the American population, what have been their contributions to American society? In 2017, I came across another book, *Muslims and the Making of America*. The author, Amir Hussain (2016) makes a bold statement, "There has never been an America without Muslims." Beginning from the history of slavery when Muslims were transported from the Old World to America, Hussain brings our attention to the rich contributions made by Muslim Americans in the fields of music, sports, and culture. The present book tries to follow the same approach. We start our journey in Chapter 2, not in the United States but in the Caribbean Islands, where Indians were transported by the British in the form of indentured laborers. We then move on to Indian activism against the British Raj in North America. Chapter 3 and Chapter 4 present a survey of Hindu Americans' contributions to music, healthcare, and education in the K-12 school systems. Chapter 5 focuses on the history of Jains in North America. Chapter 6 highlights Indian Americans' attempts to participate in civic engagement. Appendices 1–6 spotlight various aspects of Indian Americans' contributions to American life.

There are already other books that describe various Hindu movements, e.g., *Homegrown Gurus: From Hinduism in America to American Hinduism* (Gleig and Williamson 2014) and *Gurus in America* (Forsthoefel and Humes 2005). However, I wanted to survey the aspects of Indian culture that are not sufficiently described when books are written about Hindu Americans or even Indian Americans, although it is widely acknowledged that many Hindu religious ideas overlap or at least influence Indian classical music and Ayurveda. Almost all the titles mentioned above are lacking any reference to Indian classical music or Ayurveda making inroads into the Americas. Amanda Lucia (2014) in her book and Marianne Qvortrup Fibiger and Sammy Bishop (2018) in her interview about Amma, "the hugging guru," describe the tenuous relationship between Amma's Euro-American followers and her Indian followers. Hugh Urban (2016) notes a similar tension between the Euro-American and Indian followers of Osho. In my observations on Indian classical music and Ayurvedic practitioners, I discovered identical kinds of debates and discussions among the Euro-American practitioners of Indian music and Ayurveda. This book dedicates one chapter each to Indian classical music (Chapter 4) and Ayurveda and Indian doctors (Chapter 5). Some of the other publications, such as that by Kurien (2007), note how some Hindu Americans have challenged the portrayal of Hinduism in textbooks but none of them have paid any attention to the grassroots activism by Indian Americans attempting to enter the local School Boards across the United States (Chapter 6).

Similarly, the history of Jains is often glossed over or ignored when Hindus in America are described by the various authors mentioned above, although Buddhists and Sikhs are given more attention, the two other religious groups originating from India. Overall, this book is about the Indian cultural elements that are emerging and merging in mainstream America, including Indian classical music and Ayurveda. Also, the book describes one of the most ancient religious communities, the Jains, who are fast becoming Americans with their tens of dozens of temples and other organizations across North America (Chapter 5). Indians are among the most highly educated racial or ethnic groups in America (DeSilver 2014) and they are now also becoming active participants in educational leadership in K-12 School Boards across America, as described in Chapter 6 in this book.

The name of India has been linked with America since its inception due to the confusion of Christopher Columbus about the New World (Morgan 2009).

This "nominal" connection is still evident in many place names and even people of the Americas that are still named after India, e.g., the state of Indiana, Indiana University, and many Native American groups who are called Indians. After this earliest name-sake connection with India, the next significant links to India and its philosophy were established, starting in the 1800s by the transcendentalists, most notably, H. D. Thoreau, Ralph W. Emerson, Walt Whitman, and T. S. Eliot (Altman 2016). In Chapter 2, I will trace some of these early developments that brought India and its philosophy to America.

Some significant figures who have helped raise Americans' awareness about India and its culture have been leaders, such as Dr. Martin Luther King who visited Mahatma Gandhi's Ashrams in India in 1959 and brought the message of nonviolence back to the Civil Rights Movement in America (Lakshmi 2009). This book does not discuss this topic as there are several other works on this theme, such as *Mahatma Gandhi and Martin Luther King Jr: The Power of Nonviolent Action (Cultures of Peace)* (King 1999). We will see a few references to Mahatma Gandhi and the Civil Rights Movement's emphasis on nonviolence in Chapter 5 on the Jains in the Americas.

Other significant figures include George Harrison, the prominent member of the Beatles rock band, who brought Hindu ideas into his music and his life and whose ashes were scattered on Indian sacred rivers, according to the Hindu last rites. Chapter 4 on music presents some more details of his musical contributions to American music, in addition to many other maestros, such as Ravi Shankar, Ali Akbar Khan, Allah Rakha, and Zakir Hussain. Then there are Hollywood celebrities, such as Richard Gere and Julia Roberts who have embraced Buddhist and Hindu ideas, respectively. However, Hollywood is also beyond the scope of this book.

Kotkin's "Greater India" prophecy (1994) continues to be fulfilled as Indians have now emerged as the largest, most affluent, and most educated diaspora across the world (Sims, 2016). Especially from the 1990s onwards, hundreds of thousands of Indian computer engineers have entered America on H1B visas (Cockrell 2017). Their arrival, *en masse*, fueled the mushrooming of Indian temples, grocery stores, restaurants, and residential communities across North America (Eck 2001; Lessinger 1995; Levitt 2007), especially in the suburban areas of California, New York, New Jersey, Dallas, Houston, Chicago, Seattle, Atlanta, and parts of Florida. Indians have founded more start-ups than the next seven immigrant groups combined, including those from Britain, China, Taiwan, and Japan. Many Indians have been attributed with the development of everyday products and services such as Hotmail, Universal Serial Bus, Intel's Pentium microchip, and Bose speakers, to name a few. As of 2019, Indian Americans are now heading the global corporate giants, such as Microsoft, Google, Adobe, PepsiCo, and MasterCard. However, this theme has also been covered in the works by Varma (2006) and Chakravorty et al. (2017), so we do not discuss this topic either. Another economic contribution by Indians is their entrepreneurial success in the American hotel industry as explained excellently in *Life Behind the Lobby:*

Indian American Motel Owners and the American Dream (Dhingra 2012). However, the fact that Indians are also the highest number of doctors from a non-US country seems to have gone mostly unnoticed in the books about the Indian diaspora mentioned above. Hence, I devote Chapter 3 to the issues faced by Indian doctors. In that chapter, I also discuss the problems related to the practice of the ancient Indian healthcare system Ayurveda in America, another less-mentioned topic in most Indian diaspora books. Finally, Chapter 6 provides a glimpse into the issues related to the new demographic development in America and how Indian Americans are now emerging as leaders in the K-12 education segment of American society also.

As noted by Warikoo (2011), Indian immigrants differ from prior waves of immigrants from European countries and are included with other racial minorities, such as Chinese immigrants in the United States. In his analysis of Indians in America, R. K. Narayan (1985, cited in Kumar 2003) noted some interesting aspects of Indians as a minority group in America. We get a glimpse of Indians as they lived in America before the 1990s tech boom. Narayan lamented that an Indian in America was "a rather lonely being" who did not "make any attempt to integrate into American cultural or social life." As the numbers of Indians were low then, Narayan observed that on weekends, they would have to drive for "fifty miles or more towards another Indian family to eat an Indian dinner." Certainly much has changed in the lives of Indians since Narayan wrote that account of Indians in America. As of 2019, we find many Indians integrating with American society and politics at almost every level and dozens of towns across America; they have to drive just a couple of miles or less to find another Indian family for their social gatherings, not 50 miles! Narayan hopes "that the next generation of Indians (America-grown) will do better by accepting the American climate spontaneously or in the alternative return to India." While few Indians are forced to return to India due to their visa issues or other urgent reasons, most of the others and their next generations have continued to thrive in America in various ways.

In her article in *The New York Times* on September 22, 1996, cited in Kumar (2004), Bharati Mukherjee shares the debate that she had with her sister Mira. While Mira prefers to live in America as an expatriate Indian (also known as a "Non-Resident Indian"), Bharati went ahead and put her "roots down, to vote and make the difference that one can" and became an American citizen After the more than two decades since she wrote that, Indians are continuing to put more roots down and contribute to all spheres of American society, as we will see in the next few chapters. We first take a look at the history of the Indians (and the Indian culture) in the Caribbean islands and in the United States where they arrived more than a century ago.

2 Before "coolies," beyond "cyber coolies"

Indians: the silent minority

Although most contemporary scholarly discussions about the Indian migration seem to focus on the movement of Indians to foreign locations, Indians have been migrating to different regions of South Asia for centuries, as Chinmay Tumbe notes in his book *India Moving* (2018). He traces the histories of people moving from different parts of India to Myanmar during the British Raj and returning to their native locations after the 1940s. People from Uttarakhand, Rajasthan, Gujarat, Kerala, Bihar, and many other states have been moving to more lucrative parts of India for centuries. In his opinion, the scale at which Indians have been moving within India and outside India is unmatched by any other country.

Written before the Indians' influx of the late 1990s into the United States, Ravindra K. Jain, in his chapter, "Overseas Indian Communities and Relevant Theories" reviews some assimilation theories (1993). The first approaches deal with cultural persistence under the general rubric of acculturation. This kind of research involves the immigrants and how they "retain, reconstitute, and revitalize their culture" in their new host country. The second kind of theory focuses on the adaptation by immigrants in their new host country, the other side of their new life, and a new identity. The third perspective is of studying the intermixing of the host culture and immigrant culture that happened to some extent in Guyana but not in Fiji and elsewhere. Finally, he presents the Indian diaspora as an especially underprivileged sector of the global population as it used to be socio-economically weak until the 1980s. Today, Indians have radically transformed their image and are now often called "the other 1%" with the highest median family income and highest educational qualifications.

America now is home to approximately five million Indian Americans who either were born in continental America or have immigrated from India or other countries. Some of the earliest such arrivals, however, happened in the Caribbean countries, in the nineteenth century, who were termed "coolies," as shown in the 2002 BBC film, *Coolies: How Britain Re-Invented Slavery* (Sehgal, 2002). Another recent wave of arrivals happened in and after the 1990s in North America and these Indians were termed "cyber coolies" (Varma 2002), as they worked in IT industries. However, long before the coolies and cyber coolies, India had already established an indelible mark on America that remains carved in stone in various names of American places such as Indiana. Moreover, if we expand our definition of America to include the entire North, South, and Central America, the Caribbean countries are sometimes referred to as "West Indies." As is now well known, the Caribbean countries were some of the earliest lands to receive the "East Indians" in the nineteenth century when hundreds of thousands of indentured laborers arrived to work in sugar plantations.

America: the India of Columbus

As Nico Slate (2019) notes, both India and America are names given by outsiders to these two countries. The Caribbean region was named the "West Indies" in the fifteenth century when, as is well known, one of the earliest European explorers, Christopher Columbus, landed in the Bahamas and was convinced that his voyage to India had succeeded (Morgan 2009). This "Indies" word is the earliest recorded connection that India had with the New World. It was this fascination with India that urged Columbus to undertake his voyage and that eventually led to various parts of the New World being named after India, e.g., the West Indies, the US state of Indiana, Indiana University, and "American Indians." The name of the River Sindhu (or the Greek/Roman equivalent "Indus"), once defined the residents of that region who were (and are) called Hindus, thus reached the New World as well. The land of the Hindus was called Hindustan and India. Also, Columbus, unintentionally, brought the River Sindhu (Indus) to the New World. Amir Hussain makes a bold claim in his 2016 monograph: "There has never been an America without Muslims." Based on Columbus' connection between America and India, perhaps one can at least say that the very "discovery" of America happened because of India, or as it was known then "the land of the Hindoos." The desire to find "a passage to India" was so strong that a Missouri Senator, Thomas Hart Brenton, hoped that perhaps a railroad link could be established to India, as mentioned on his statue in Lafayette Park in St. Louis, "There is the East; there is India."

Valerie Flint (2017) (cited in Prashad 2000) notes the earliest references to India in various texts that Columbus had referred as he prepared for his journeys. Columbus imagined India to be the land of exotica, full of pygmies where "the giants of the Vulgate Genesis 6:4" could be placed (by way of proselytization that is). In one of the maps, India was shown with a monster with eyes in his chest. According to Flint (2017, 95), Columbus imagined India

> subdued by Alexander, contained 5,000 towns and nine nations, was filled with great standing armies and huge numbers of elephants and horses and covered one-third of the surface of the habitable earth. It has mountains made of gold. Off its coasts stand the islands of "Patale," "Chryse," "Argire," and "Taprobane," rich in gold, silver, pearls and precious stones.

Flint goes on to mention that Columbus imagined,

> India was also, according to Solinus, the home of a tribe of women founded by the daughter of Hercules who, like Amazons, forswore the rule of men. There were monstrous beasts in these parts also; the man-eating Mantichore (perhaps based upon the cheetah), with a triple row of teeth in his human head, a lion's body, a hissing voice like that of a serpent, a scorpion's tail and a tremendous speed of movement; the giant black eel; the huge swimming snakes capable of devouring stags; the bulls with turning horns; and elephant's feet; the two-armed sea serpents that pull elephants under water; whales that cover four acres; the giant turtles with shells large enough to provide roofs for houses. India, according to Solinus, provided parrots too; the "psittacum" with his gorgeous plumage and hooked beak. Some of the fabulous beasts of India found secure refuge in the Medieval Bestiary; others roamed across *mappae mundi*. India was renowned also for pepper, having a great pepper forest on the southern side of the Caucasus mountains, and, of course, it provided many precious metals ("mountains of Gold") and infinite numbers of jewels.
>
> (ibid., 17)

It seems like some of the medieval stereotypes about the land of the "Hindoos" are still prevalent in our times. For instance, in the 1850s, when the rumor spread that an American lawyer Daniel Ullmann, who was running for political office, was born in Calcutta to Hindu parents, it quickly demolished his political career, and his American Party was disparaged with the label "Hindoos" (Slate 2019, 11). In 2019, Tulasi Gabbard, the first Hindu Congresswoman, was criticized for her religious heritage after she announced her Presidential campaign.[1]

Now, however, let us look at some theories that claim that the Chinese and even Indians might have landed in the Americas even before Columbus. For instance, The Economist published a report, "China Beat Columbus to It, Perhaps," on January 12, 2006. Cris Mahadeo and Kumar Mahabir (2005) compare several features in Indian and South and Central American cultures and civilizations and speculate that Indians may have been to those parts of the world long before Columbus.

India in the early American historical references

Jumping a few centuries later, Nico Slate (2019) finds an astonishing reference to India during the American freedom struggle. He points out that as the American War of Independence was beginning, on the other side of the globe, India's enslavement was also occurring. Lord Cornwallis was a crucial figure in both of these phenomena in what was later known as the British Empire. On October 19, 1781, Cornwallis surrendered to General George Washington. Soon after that, he was appointed as the Commander-in-Chief of British India and saw the establishment of the British Raj that continued for the next 166 years.

Slate (ibid., 29) notes another reference to India as a model civilized country by Timothy Pickering, a commissioner appointed by President George Washington in July 1791, when Pickering addressed the Iroquois Confederacy of American Indians in Newtown, New York. Pickering signed the Calico Treaty between the US government and American Indians by gifting the famous Calico cotton from India. The agreement continues to be honored by both parties today. However, another kind of Indian correlation was not accepted by the US authorities. In the early 1900s, "Indian" males were arrested when some of them formed same-sex relationships, for instance, in Sacramento, a Punjabi Indian migrant Tara Singh and his American Indian partner Hector McInnes (ibid., 21) shocked society.

In addition to these intangible and historical connections between the two regions of the world, scholars cite a "colonial diary" by Reverend William Bentley (Bentley 1962 [1905], quoted in Zia 2001). Bentley states:

> [He] had the pleasure of seeing for the first time a native of the Indies from Madras. He is of very dark complection (*sic*), long black hair, soft countenance, tall, & well proportioned. He is said to be darker than Indians in general of his own cast, being much darker than any native Indians of America. I had no opportunity to judge of his abilities, but his countenance was not expressive. He came to Salem with Capt. J. Gibaut, and has been in Europe.

We have no further details about this mysterious "Man from Madras." However, descriptions of similar "natives of Indies" arriving in the "West Indies" are abundant. Regardless of their religions, all South Asians were called "Hindoos" for at least a century (Bald 2015). Contemporary scholars of American Hinduism, such as Prema Kurien (2007) and Vasudha Narayanan (2007), have similarly followed the same practice and have used the term Hinduism to describe the earliest migration of Hindu ideas to America. Michael Altman disagrees with this practice since this assumes "Hinduism moves like a giant wooden box carried across the oceans from India to America." However, I would argue that both Kurien and Narayana are fully aware of both the varieties and diversities of countless texts and contexts within this umbrella term "Hinduism," as well as how some glimpses of those texts and contexts arrived in America. Many observers have noted the legendary arrival of St. Thomas in first-century India as the arrival of Christianity in India,[2] even though it was not the adequately packaged "box of Christianity" either. The same comment applies to the case of the arrival of "Islam" in India[3] or many other religions in different parts of the world. No religion is transplanted to a foreign location as an adequately packaged box but gets slowly diffused across a long and flexible timescale, especially if the religion has no explicit proselytizing mission, such as Hinduism. Altman goes on to argue that Hinduism (and religion) remain problematic categories in contemporary academic discussions, but that can be said perhaps for all other such labels, such as Christianity, Shinto,

Daoism, Confucianism, or Buddhism, as also noted by Andrea Jain in her book, *Selling Yoga* (2015) and by Long in his book, *Hinduism in America* (2020).

Similarly, the label of another minority Indian tradition, Jainism, has been questioned (Flügel 2005). All such tags continue to serve their purposes across the world today among academics and the general public (Jones 2019). Notably, the academics of each such tradition acknowledge the problems of such labels and yet continue to employ them in their research and teaching, perhaps for lack of an alternative method to be able to refer to all the diversities. However, some common elements continue to bind each tradition under one umbrella term. More discussion on this topic is beyond the scope of this book.

Indian American connections during the British Raj

As we noted earlier, the legendary wealth of India lured Columbus but he ended up in the New World. Interestingly, some of that wealth of India did reach the United States in a different form and via a different route – via the United Kingdom during the British Raj. For instance, Yale University received its name from one of its earliest donors, Elihu Yale,[4] a Welsh merchant, who made his fortune as the President of the East India Company settlement in Fort St. George at Madras. The school officially became Yale College in 1718, when it was renamed in his honor when he donated the funds after selling "two trunks of textiles (mostly Indian muslins, calico, poplins, silk crepe and camlet which he brought." Another milestone that celebrated "the wealth of India" was in 1825 when the East India Marine Society of Salem (EIMS) inaugurated its East India Marine Hall with President John Quincy Adams as their guest. EIMS, established in 1799,[5] brought materials collected from India, such as images of Hindu deities and other items from temples and ascetics. In 1791, almost the entire revenue of the United States depended on the maritime trade with India. In the early nineteenth century, an active business of goods continued to flourish between India and America, and in 1807, imports from India totaled over $4 million (Altman 2017). In 1797, Jacob Crowninshield brought an elephant named "Old Bet" in a ship that became an exotic circus display in Boston (Kamath 1998). Although many of the goods of EIMS constructed an exotic, obsolete, and "the cradle of the world" image of India, later transcendentalists in another Boston suburb, Concord, provided an alternate philosophical and literary image of India devoid of the "superstitions" or "idols."

Early literary portrayals of India in America

In 1784, another critical contribution to the understanding of religions of India came from Boston when Hannah Adams published a significant survey of world's religions, *A View of Religions*, the first publication by an American woman. *A View of Religions* and her other works are regarded as the stimuli for the beginning of the discipline of comparative religions in various American universities and elsewhere in the nineteenth century and later. This work was also the first ever account of Hinduism written by an American, although it was almost entirely based on the reports of her British counterparts (Altman 2017).

Polymath Joseph Priestley's *A Comparison of the Institutions of Moses with Those of the Hindoos and Other Ancient Nations*, published in 1799, in Philadelphia, was the next major work that attempted to study Hinduism (ibid.). An electronic copy of this book[6] shows the name of the second American President John Adams on it. Some of the notes by Adams are also present in the first three sections of the book. As far as we know, this must be the first American book with Hindoo in its title. Although John Adams, the second President, tried to learn about the Hindoos from this book, most of the other early political and religious leaders of America made no mention of Hinduism or Buddhism, although some of them, such as Benjamin Franklin, openly included Muslims in some of their speeches and texts, as noted by Muslim leader Eboo Patel (2018). However, Patel, in his book on interfaith issues, did not include Hindus but focused only on Muslims.

Kamath (1998) cites several other crucial contributions and influences that India made during the British Raj. For instance, in 1805, Boston's *The Monthly Anthology* published the famous Sanskrit play *Shakuntalam*'s in a translation by William Jones, the British Orientalist and founder of the Asiatic Society. Boston also had other books about Indian culture available such as the translation of *Ramayana* and William Ward's *A View of the History, Literature, and Mythology of the Hindus*, published by Serampore Mission Press in 1818. One of the pioneering transcendentalists, Ralph Waldo Emerson read these books at Harvard Library in 1847.[7] A work was published in 1804 in Calcutta by Henry Colebrook, *Remarks on the Husbandry and Internal Commerce of Bengal*. In 1828, in his dictionary, Noah Webster added the entry for HIN'DOO, and in the 1849 and 1864 editions, the entry was extended to HIN'DOO-ISM, HIN'DU-ISM (Altman 2017, xii).

In addition to the genuine curiosity about India and its traditions, there was also a missionary urge to "save" the *heathen* Indians, for instance, in Cotton Mather's *India Christina* (1721). He sent some books to India and received the Tamil translation of the New Testament. In the footsteps of Richard King and Edward Said, Altman (ibid.) also notes that such accounts exoticized and otherized Indian and other traditions and helped form a national and religious identity of America. The first wave of missionaries who visited India were trained at Andover Seminary, cofounded by Jedidiah Morse in 1807 in the Boston area. Around the same time, Morse also cofounded the American Board of Commission for Foreign Missions (ABCFM) that sent those missionaries and the magazine, *The Panoplist*, later renamed *The Missionary Herald*, that published the reports from such missions. In 1812, the first missionary batch arrived in Bombay (now Mumbai). One prominent missionary story, "Fragment of a Vision," was published in

Massachusetts Missionary Magazine in one of its issues in 1807. Another leading missionary letter was by Claudius Buchanan, a British East India chaplain, that was reprinted widely in the evangelical publications of New England. The letter contained one of the earliest and most exoticized accounts of Puri's Jagannath Yatra and coined the new English term "juggernaut." In 1811, he wrote *Christian Researchers in Asia* that further informed American missionaries about Hindu practices through a Biblical perspective. Following in the footsteps of Buchanan, later American missionaries also continued to portray Hinduism as a "bloody, licentious, noisy, superstitious, and Catholic religion," and as the "antithesis of true Protestant religion that was spiritual, rational, ordered, abstract, and systematized" (ibid.), similar to what Partha Mitter (2013) found in European accounts of India.

Indic ideas in America through Raja Ram Mohan Roy and the Transcendentalists

As Kamath (1998) notes, the first Indian to influence Americans was Raja Ram Mohan Roy, whose interpretation of Christianity found its commentators in influential American religious publications such as *The Christian Register*. Roy's books such as *The Precepts of Jesus* (1820), *Second Appeal to the Christian Public in Defence of the Precepts of Jesus* (1822), and *A Vindication of the Incarnation of the Deity as a Common Basis of Hinduism and Christianity* (1833) were reprinted in America multiple times. American libraries acquired them, and reviewers, such as William Tudor (1818) wrote, "Ram Mohun Roy is not a Christian, it is true, but the doctrine he inculcates differs very little from the Christian doctrine repeating the nature and attributes of the Deity. It is the same in its spirit and objects." Roy corresponded with many American intellectuals via mail and met many in person during his trip to England. According to Adrienne Moore's 1942 book *Rammohun Roy and America*, Roy was instrumental in piquing the curiosity about India in many New Englanders, such as Emerson and his associates (Kamath 1998). Altman also notes the influence of Roy on both sides of the Protestant disputes, the Trinitarians and the Unitarians, who both published excerpts from Roy's introduction in his *Translation of an Abridgement of the Vedant*. Both sides tried to interpret Roy's reformation of Hinduism in their version of Protestant Christianity. After his death, locks of his hair were used for fund-raising for the abolitionist cause in 1844 since he remained an icon for liberal theology and social reform for over two decades, as seen in more than two hundred magazine articles in 31 journals and magazines (Altman 2017).

While Roy was influencing some sections of American society, the school textbooks continued to portray India and its religions as the exotic other, as noted by Altman (ibid.) in the books written by Samuel Goodrich, aka Peter Parley and by S. Augustus Mitchell. Mitchell in his book, *A System of Modern Geography* (1844), Goodrich in his *A System of School Geography* (1833), and Parley in his *Geography for Beginners* (1845) maintained a hierarchy of races, religions, and society in which Europeans are placed first before other races such as Asians, Native Americans, and Africans. Only Western Europeans and Americans were fully civilized and "enlightened" in this hierarchy. Similarly, many textbooks mentioned monotheistic religions as "true" religions while Hinduism and all the rest were clubbed together as "Pagan or Heathen" religions, following in the footsteps of early missionary writings, such as by Hannah Adams. Hindoos were "brown, half-civilized, pagan, and inferior" to "white, Protestant, and enlightened" Americans, according to these textbooks. Similarly, *The Tales of Peter Parley about Asia* (1845), *Lights and Shadows of Asiatic History* (1844), and *The World and Its Inhabitants* (1856) described the Hindu caste system, children and women, religious practices, and beliefs as violent, immoral, and superstitious. In their *Progressive Third Reader* (1857), Salem Town and Nelson M. Holbrook taught the "Theory of Rain" by citing a dialogue between a Hindu child and the Scottish missionary Alexander Duff, to show how Hindu child accepts his "superstition" about his Hindu rain god Indra and is ready to take Christianity as the enlightened option. Many portions of the books tried to glorify the British administration for its "civilizing mission." In addition, magazines such as *Harper's New Monthly* also exoticized India and other foreign cultures to entertain and inform its American readers of their Protestant superiority, for instance, in its 1853 article, "Ghosts and Sorceresses of India," the 1885 story, "A Priest of Doorga," the 1857 article, "Madras, in Pictures", the 1867 article, "Calcutta, the City of Palaces," and the 1878 article "Juggernaut" (Altman 2017).

Quite different from the portrayal of India and its culture in missionary accounts, textbooks, and magazines, the metaphysical religion of American Transcendentalism brought the more philosophical and literary aspects of India to America. Ralph Waldo Emerson (1803–1882) was indeed profoundly influenced by Indic ideas from his study of texts, translated by the British Orientalists, such as Narayaṇa, Code of Manu, *Bhagavad Gītā, Vishṇu Purāṇa, Bhāgavata Purāṇa*, and the *Upaniṣads*. Hindu ideas influenced some of the poems he composed, such as "Hamatreya," "Brahma," "Maya," and his essays such as "Illusions." Decades later, his granddaughter Gertrude Emerson Sen married an Indian. Emerson's younger colleague, Henry David Thoreau (1817–1862) left an everlasting legacy in the form of his influence on Mahatma Gandhi in the Indian freedom struggle. Like Emerson, Thoreau also read several Indic texts in translation such as *The Laws of Manu, Bhagavad Gītā, Dharma Shastra, Shakuntalam, Samkhya Karika, Vishnu Purāna, Hitopadesha*, and *Harivansa*. He is also remembered for his unique experiment of living like an Indic Yogi by Walden pond (Kamath 1998). The same Walden pond had already made at least one connection to India (Slate 2019, 46), when hundreds of tons of ice were shipped from this pond in Massachusetts and exported to several Indian cities provided a beautiful metaphor to Thoreau when he stated "I bathe in the Indian philosophy" and "the pure Walden water is mingled with the sacred water of the Ganges" (ibid., 31). Such was the influence of these Transcendentalists on later religious movements such as Universal Unitarians that Diana Eck calls the former ancestors to the latter in the documentary *The Asian & Abrahamic Religions: A Divine Encounter in America* (2011). However, since Thoreau quoted Raja Ram Mohan Roy in his *Walden* (Altman 2017), perhaps we can regard Roy as one of the ancestors of the Transcendentalists. Another influence on the Transcendentalists can be seen in Swami Vivekananda and later transnational gurus, such as Osho. Following in the footsteps of the Transcendentalists, they often described the West as scientific, active, and masculine and the East as spiritual, contemplative, and feminine. Instead of criticizing either side, these gurus sought to integrate both as two complementary sides of human civilization. The comparative perspectives of the Transcendentalists continued with the efforts of James Freeman Clarke's liberal and mystical Christianity, Lydia Maria Child's religious liberalism, and Samuel Johnson's Universal Religion. They also coined and utilized the category of Brahamanism, as the Indian religion, in these efforts. Decades later, under the influence of William James, the comparative religion project would culminate in the launch of the formal comparative religions discipline in America (ibid.). In 2018, when I visited the home where Emerson and Thoreau spent several years reading and discussing India, I could not see any prominent memory of their connection with India except a glimpse of some of the Indian books that they read.

Similar to the Transcendentalists, Helena Blavatsky also sought to mine the wisdom tradition of India and integrate the two opposite poles of science and religion when she, with Henry Steel Olcott, co-founded the Theosophical Society in 1875. In 1877, in her major two-volume work, *Isis Unveiled: A Master-Key to the Ancient and Modern*, she wrote (Blavatsky 1877, 9) "In the Vedas, for instance, we find positive proof that so long ago as 2,000 b.c. the Hindu sages and scholars must have been acquainted with the rotundity of our globe and the heliocentric system." She continued, "That it is to India, the country less explored, and less known than any other, that all the other great nations of the world are indebted for their languages, arts, legislature, and civilization" (ibid., 125). However, this comparative project was challenged and resisted by Arya Samaj's founder, Swami Dayanand Saraswati, whom Blavatsky and Olcott tried to co-opt into the wisdom religion. In 1889, a Theosophical Society member, William Quan Judge, published perhaps the first ever American interpretation of Patanjali's Yoga Sutras, *The Yoga Aphorisms of Patanjali* (Altman 2017).

Other Indic-inspired intellectuals of that period include Amos Bronson Alcott (1799–1888), who was a pioneer in adopting vegetarianism and organic food. He was also instrumental in reprinting Edwin Arnold's "The Light of Asia," a long poem on the life of the Buddha that ran into 83 editions. An American Quaker poet and abolitionist, John Greenleaf Whittier (1807–1892) was a poet inspired by Indic ideas that he found from his reading of texts such as the *Bhagavad Gītā*, "The Light of Asia," and *Sacred Books of the East*. Hermann Melville (1819–1891) was aware of Lord Vishnu and other Indic ideas that he referenced in his work *Moby Dick*. The last contemporary name in this group is Walt Whitman (1819–1892), who had also read the *Bhagavad Gītā* and other Indic texts that are reflected in his works, such as *Passage to India* (Kamath 1998). In 1841, John Christian Frederick Heyer, the first Lutheran missionary, preferred Indians in India over American Indians and remained in India for one of the most extended periods for any American minister of that era (Slate 2019, 58).

One of the earliest American Indological efforts was the establishment of the American Oriental Society in 1842. The first American Sanskrit scholars were Edward Elbridge Salisbury (1814–1901) at Yale and Fitz Edward Hall (1825–1901) at Harvard. Hall went to India to find his brother, taught Sanskrit in Banaras, and edited the Sanskrit text *Vishnu Purana*. Salisbury's student William Dwight Whitney (1827–1901) became a Sanskrit professor at Yale in 1854 and wrote the first American book on Sanskrit grammar (1879). After Whitney, Edward Washburn Hopkins (1857–1932) taught at Yale and published *The Religions of India* (1895).

Meanwhile, many others, including James Bradstreet Greenough (1833–1900) and Charles Rockwell Lanman (1850–1941), taught Sanskrit at Harvard University. Lanman's books included the *Sanskrit Reader* and *Beginnings of Hindu Pantheism*, and he edited the *Harvard Oriental Series*. Other major Indologists of that time included Maurice Bloomfield (1855–1928), A. V. William Jackson (1862–1937), Franklin Edgerton (1885–1963), W. Norman Brown (1892–1975), and Joseph Campbell (1904–1987). Lanman's student T. S. Eliot (1888–1965) received the Nobel Prize for Literature in 1948. His works, *The Waste Land, Four Quarters, Ash Wednesday,* and *Murder in the Cathedral,* show the Indic influence from his reading of the *Upanishads,* the *Bhagavad Gītā,* and *Yoga Sutras.* Like Eliot, the novelist, Christopher Isherwood developed his ideas based on Indic philosophy that he learned from the *Upanishads,* as taught by his guru Swami Prabhavananda of the Vedanta Society of Southern California in Hollywood. Both also collaborated on several scholarly projects, including the translation of the *Bhagavad Gītā* (Kamath 1998).

In 1880, even as the influence of Transcendentalism was ending, a geologist Clarence Edward Dutton named several Grand Canyon features after Hindu deities, such as Brahma Temple, Vishnu Temple, Shiva Temple, and the Hindu Amphitheatre (*Hinduism Today,* August 1987). And in 1945, Robert Oppenheimer similarly described the first nuclear test with a famous verse from the *Bhagavad Gītā* (11.32) "Now I am become Death, the destroyer of worlds." In 1870, 586 people who were born in India were in the USA, and by 1900, this number stood at 2,031 (Chakravorty et al. 2017). In the 1910 census, they were referred to as "Hindus," and numbered 2,545 then. By the 1940 census, their number had decreased to 2,405. In 1883, two Indian ladies, who were also cousins, came to the USA. They were Anandi Gopal Joshi and Pandita Ramabai. Anandi Joshi and another Indian woman, Kadambini Ganguly became the first two Indian medical doctors in the USA (ibid.). As Slate notes (2019, 13), around this time, the "Indian" category worked as an orientalist category to differentiate White Americans from non-Whites.

Meanwhile, when the American humorist Mark Twain visited Varanasi in 1896, he criticized the British Raj but was charmed by Indian spirituality (Twain 1929, 494), "Benares is a religious Vesuvius. In its bowels, the theological forces have been heaving and tossing, rumbling, thundering and quaking, boiling, and weltering and flaming and smoking for ages." In 1902, one of the most prominent American inventors, Thomas Alva Edison, was also charmed by Indic spirituality in New Jersey. He became a member of the Theosophical Society and made a film *The Hindoo Fakir*, showing mystical and magical Hindu practices (Krell et al. 2011).

Influx and influence of Indians as indentured laborers in the Caribbean

On March 21, 1916, the British colonial government abolished the Indian indentureship system with effect from March 21, 1917. In more than 70 years of indentureship, more than 400,000 Indians had arrived in the Caribbean countries, and today that number stands at more than a million. And since this time, Indians have influenced the local culture, religion, food, music, architecture, politics, and economy in a significant way (Mahabir 2006).

One of the earliest notable political accomplishments was in Guyana when Chhedi Jagan became the Chief Minister (1953), then Premiere (1961–1964), and finally the fourth President of Guyana (1992–1997). His wife Janet Jagan became the next President after his death. When she resigned, Bharrat Jagdeo became the next President of Guyana until 2011 when he left by setting up the term limit for the Guyanese Presidents. In Trinidad, Basdeo Panday became the fifth Prime Minister of Trinidad and Tobago from 1995 to 2001. Kamla Persad-Bissessar was the next Indian who became the seventh Prime Minister of Trinidad and Tobago from 2010 to 2015. She was the country's first female Prime Minister (Clarke 1986; 1991; 1993). In Suriname, Ramsewak Shankar became the fourth President from 1988 to 1990.

One of the most noticeable impacts of the Indian presence in Trinidad and Tobago is the celebration of Divali (the spelling that is used in the Caribbean, although Diwali is the spelling used elsewhere). It was Hans Hanoomansingh, the President of the National Council of Indian Culture (NCIC) in 1986, who inspired the creation of a new Divali Nagar (the City of Lights). Divali has been celebrated as a national holiday since 1966, and it has now emerged as the second largest festival that is celebrated by all ethnic groups in Trinidad and Tobago. Other Hindu groups such as the Fireburn Mandir, Hindu Prachar Kendra, Edinburgh Mandir, Beaucarro Mandir, and the McBean Mandir also supported NCIC. Divali Nagar was established in the parking lot of Seeram Brothers at the Mid Centre Mall in Chaguanas, the fastest-growing borough in Trinidad and Tobago. This first celebration recorded more than 23,000 people present. Over more than two decades, Divali Nagar has showcased Indian food and culture in Trinidad and Tobago and elsewhere consistently, including glimpses of the unique lifestyle of the Caribbean, musical performances by local as well as Indian artists, and following themes of globally renowned Indian leaders such as Mahatma Gandhi and Swami Vivekananda. In 1991, the government of Trinidad and Tobago granted the NCIC 30 acres of land to develop the Divali Nagar facility and for other community activities (www.ncictt.com/2012-04-14-11-07-13/achievements; accessed July 8, 2017).

As already mentioned, Hindus comprise the second largest religious group after Christians in Trinidad and Tobago, Guyana, and Suriname. And this is reflected in various Hindu temples that have altered the landscape of these countries. For instance, the "Temple in the Sea" at Waterloo in Trinidad that Sewdass Sadhu built singlehandedly over more than two decades, by carrying the building materials on his bicycle. One of the most significant Hindu temples is Dattatreya Yoga Center that installed an 85-feet-high Hanuman statue in 2003. Hindu women are also increasingly leading various recitation and ritual activities in Trinidad and Tobago (Mahabir 2006).

As mentioned earlier, Guyana was the home of the earliest Indian indentured laborers in 1838. According to Peter Ruhomon (1988 [1947], 259), one of the earliest Hindu temples was discovered when the Royal Commission visited the colony in 1870 (it was then known as British Guiana). By 1890, the settlement had 33 Hindu temples, and 43 by 1917. Today, in the Caribbean region, there are hundreds of Hindu temples of different styles, such as timber-made single-chamber, or octagonal shapes made of concrete , or pagoda styled ones (Mahabir 2006).

Perhaps the most influential Hindu organization in the Caribbean region is the Sanatan Dharma Maha Sabha (SDMS), founded by Bhadase Sagan Maraj in 1952. SDMS manages more than 150 Hindu temples, more than 50 schools (including a girls' college), and runs its own radio station and TV channel. In Guyana, Saraswati Vidya Niketan, a Hindu secondary school, that opened in 2002, has achieved excellent academic results.

In Guyana, Reepu Daman Persaud established the Guyana Hindu Dharmic Sabha (GHDS) on January 8, 1974.[8] He remained the President of the Sabha until his death in April 2013. Since its inception, the Sabha has conducted diverse programs and events that cater to the needs of Hindus in Guyana. The Sabha comprises eight branches and has over 125 affiliated temples throughout the country, mostly supported by its younger members, especially women. The GHDS also conducts various programs in education, health, Indian music, languages, Indian cuisine, and the welfare of women and children. Hindu festivals are celebrated with much fanfare by GHDS as well.

In Suriname, Sanatan Dharma Maha Sabha and Gayatri Mandir have been at the forefront of conducting Hindu festivals. Also, Arya Samaj inspired Arya Dewaker, recognized as a cultural association by the Dutch authorities in 1930, which plays an essential role in Suriname. In 2013, it celebrated the 80th anniversary of its orphanage. It manages a major Hindu temple in Paramaribo and more than a dozen other temples across Suriname. It also runs about a dozen schools. Hindus still speak Sarnami Hindustani, a unique dialect of the North Indian language Bhojpuri in Suriname (*Hinduism*

Today, January 16, 2002) and this has helped the community maintain cultural traditions because, unlike the British custom elsewhere, the Dutch did not force their language or religion on others (Mahabir 2001). While Burg and van der Veer (1986) and van der Veer and Vertovec (1991) paint Suriname with the same broad-brush stroke with its neighboring countries such as Trinidad and Guyana, Algoe (2011), Dew (1975), and Choenni (2016) provide deeper insights into Surinamese Hinduism. Hindus in Suriname have been more fortunate as they faced much less oppression and discrimination than their counterparts in Trinidad. Ramsoedh and Bloemberg (2001) also reach a similar conclusion. Algoe further cites Pew Research to show that Suriname today is one of the most religiously diverse countries in the world. Despite the dominance of Christianity during the colonial period there, similar to that in Trinidad and Guyana, religious pluralism and diversity are flourishing in Suriname. Arya (1968) presented another important study on Hindus in Suriname is by providing insights into the Hindu ritual songs and folk songs there.

According to Mahabir (2006), other noticeable influences of Hindus' presence are in the local flora and fauna in Caribbean countries. Plants such as the Tulsi (*Ocimum sanctum*), neem (*Azadirachta indica*), and Peepul (*Ficus religiosa*) are planted by Hindus, wherever they live. The British brought animals such as the domesticated cattle and water buffalo to use them as traction animals during the indentureship. Similarly, the small Indian mongoose helped to control the rats that infested the sugar cane plantations in Jamaica and other Caribbean islands. The Indian presence also transformed the local cuisine by introducing food such as the "doubles" sandwiches. In my research, I came across a 2007 honors thesis by Vincent E. Burgess at the Ohio State University. Citing Mansingh and Mansingh (1999), the thesis claims that Hinduism influenced the founder of the Rastafarian community in Jamaica, Leonard Howell:

> Before Howell began spreading the Rastafarian message, he became friends with an Indian man named Laloo, who served as his bodyguard ... Laloo is credited with giving Howell a Hindu identity by changing his name to Gagunguru Maragh (aka Gong Maragh, the Tough King, or Tough Gong) ... The giving of a new name is characteristic of initiation into Hinduism, and it is highly possible that Laloo was acting as a sort of guru to Howell ... taking on a new name is still practiced today in many Rastafarian sects.

> Laloo is also credited with the introduction of many mystical Hindu beliefs, practices, and language into Rastafarian philosophy and prayers. Early Rastafarian prayers contained many Hindi, Bengali, and Urdu words, and are believed to have been chanted in "Hindu mantra style." ...

> The Rastafarian use of the word 'Jah,' to refer to both God and Haile Selassie, is popularly believed to have biblical origins as a shortened form of either Jehovah or Yahweh. Although a biblical connection does reinforce its usage, the Mansinghs believe that it was originally derived from

the Hindu term *'Jai'* (victory). ... As Ras Tafari gained the status of African Lord Rama/Krishna during the 1940s, phonetic usage of the word Jai was continued. But Rama, Krishna, and Kali were replaced by Ras Tafari. The Mansinghs also believe that the Rastafarian adoption of a vegetarian diet was a result of Hindu influences. Some Rastafarians hold to strict dietary restrictions, ... and many Rastas abstain from alcohol, coffee, or processed teas. Although many Indians do occasionally eat goat, lamb, or pork, most Hindus do have a predilection towards vegetarianism. The majority of sadhus, regardless of sectarian affiliation, refrain from eating meat, fish, and eggs. The consumption of such foods is believed to violate the ethical doctrine of non-violence (ahimsa). Traditional Indian dietary science believes that ganja makes the body hypersensitive to toxins associated with meat, and, subsequently, religious cultures that place a high value on the use of ganja also tend to encourage a vegetarian diet. For this reason, it is likely that the Rastafarian tendency towards a vegetarian diet also has its roots in Hinduism.

Although all of these Indian influences reinforce the notion of religious pastiche, it is the ritualistic smoking of marijuana and the growing of long, matted hair which appear to illustrate the most direct connection between the two traditions (of Hinduism and Rastafarianism).

Anthropologist Linda Ainouche reaches the same conclusion in her 2017 documentary entitled *The Dreadlocks Story*. In addition to all the above influences that Hindus had in Caribbean countries, they also started making their presence felt in other major countries in North America, such as Canada and the United States. The first wave of migration was from India to the Caribbean and the second wave from the Caribbean to England and North America. Indentured Indians came from North India and parts of South India to work on colonial plantations between 1838 and 1917 in the Caribbean. In time, those who went to Suriname went on to migrate in large numbers to Holland where they have formed distinct Sarnami communities that are Hindustani, based on religion and language.

Similarly, those in the British-controlled parts of the Caribbean went to England earlier where they too are a distinct community. Later, many from Guyana, Trinidad, and Jamaica migrated to Canada. Some Indians from Trinidad claimed refugee status. Today, large pockets (especially of Guyanese) are in New York and Florida (Melwani 1995).

One such immigrant who migrated from Trinidad to Illinois for her undergraduate studies shared this with me in Arlington, Texas, where she lives now:

People that move to areas of the USA that are not populated with people from the Caribbean with similar upbringing face an identity crisis. I identified as Indian while growing up in Trinidad, i.e., between 0–18 years of age. However, after moving to rural Illinois, where I was "one of a kind" on the campus, I was frequently asked, "What race are you?" (the

University coded me as Hispanic, and I was told by the institution that my race classification would not be changed because of the geographical location I was from). In Trinidad, I identified as Indian, I expressed this and was quickly told by the Indian students (i.e., the ones who came from India) that I could not be Indian since I was not born there (never mind my name, customs, and traditions are Indian). Hence, I adopted the Indo-Trinidadian racial term, meaning a native Trinidadian of Indian descent. My religious identity has always been and will always be Hindu. I was accepted as Hindu, and that was never questioned or challenged, probably because I would not let it be. If the census category reflected religion, I would always classify as a Hindu, and this will not change. To most folks, racial identity is seen as a reflection of birthplace instead of having an identity defined by belonging to a particular ethnic group. I think people that move to the areas of the US where there are existing Caribbean support systems do not experience such issues. For them, a safe space is available, and individuals can maintain their identities because of their affinity groups and defining one's race, and identity is not questioned.

Indian Americans and the Indian struggle for independence in America

One of the earliest examples of the political presence of Indians in the United States was when some Indian students and the Pacific Coast Indian laborers brought the Indian freedom struggle to North America. Although, initially, Americans were indifferent to the Indian freedom struggle, eventually they became interested after Irish nationalists supported the Indians. The American government, for the most part, remained in favor of the British Raj even as American people supported the Indian people's anti-colonial struggle.

The Pan-Aryan Association in the United States was co-founded in 1906 by Mohammed Barkatullah (founding president) and Samuel Louis Joshi (founding secretary), who both were inspired by Shyamji Krishna Varma, the founder of the Indian Home Rule Society in Europe. The Irish revolutionaries in the US actively supported the Pan-Aryan Association. Besides the unity between Irish and Indian people, the association also advocated unity between Hindus and Muslims. Several Americans started supporting the cause of India's freedom and established the *Indo-American National Association*, led by Myron H. Phelps. The name of this association later became *Society for the Advancement of India*.

In 1907, Shyamji's Varma's colleague, Bhikaiji Cama (aka Madame Cama) came to New York and enthusiastically supported the Indian freedom cause. She met both the Pan-Aryan Association and the Society for the Advancement of India, and influenced them to join together and agree to work together. President Theodore S. Roosevelt favored the British Raj in India, saying:

> The successful administration of India has been one of the most notable achievements of the white race during the past two centuries. If the

English control were now withdrawn from India, the whole peninsula would become chaos of bloodshed and violence.

(Rubin 2011)

Unlike the Indian students, Indian laborers had difficulties as soon as they started coming to the USA from Canada (due to discrimination there as well). In the economic crisis in 1907, they were expelled from the mills in the state of Washington and other places in the USA. In such a scenario, the *Hindustan Association* was established by Taraknath Das, Ramnath Puri, and other Indian Americans in San Francisco. Puri started publishing a nationalistic periodical *Circular-i-Azadi* that was discontinued due to the opposition to its violent messages. Puri and Barkatullah eventually left the USA and moved to Japan, but Das continued to lead the Association. Das had first come to the USA in 1906 as a student and had enrolled at the University of California at Berkeley. He later moved to the University of Washington at Seattle and earned a BA and MA in Political Science. In 1925, he received the first PhD from the School of Foreign Service at Georgetown University. He had been pursuing anti-British revolutionary activities all his life, such as launching a new periodical *The Free Hindusthan* from Canada. However, after his doctorate, he focused only on his teaching career. With his wife, Mary Keatinge Morse, he co-founded the National Association for the Advancement of Colored People, the National Woman's Party, and the Taraknath Das Foundation to foster intellectual collaborations between India and the USA. Although in 1935, US citizenship was withdrawn from Das and many other Indians, in 1946, the USA granted him (and other Indians) citizenship once more. As of 2019, his foundation still supports Indian students at Columbia University and a few other universities in the USA.

Compared to the associations described above, a couple of Sikh organization had a better impact, especially among the Sikh community in North America. One of the colleagues of Das, Teja Singh, established the *Khalsa Diwan Society* in 1907 in Vancouver. Also, in the same year, the *Pacific Coast Khalsa Diwan Society* was launched. Like the earlier mentioned revolutionaries, Singh was also inspired by Shyamji Varma. Another Punjabi revolutionary in Canada was Gurudutt Kumar, who started the newspaper *Swadesh Sewak* in Gurmukhi.

In 1911, two Indian freedom leaders, Lala Har Dayal and Thakur Das, came to North America from Paris to unite various smaller revolutionary associations (Brown 1976; Elam 2014). Har Dayal (1844–1939) had earlier renounced his Oxford scholarship under the influence of Shyamji Varma. In 1908, he returned to India but soon went to Paris and joined Madame Cama and other revolutionaries. He edited the paper *Bande Mataram* there but eventually reached the USA to give a unified voice to the disjointed Indian revolutionary groups. After teaching Indian philosophy and Sanskrit at Stanford University for a short time, he arrived at Berkeley and formed a revolutionary student group there with Indian students. Later, he moved to British Columbia and took up the issues of discrimination and exploitation of Indian laborers there. Both the Hindustan Association and Sikh Khalsa Diwan actively supported him. In 1913, he organized a meeting in which several delegates came from different places who wanted to form a unified new association to raise their voice against the British Raj. This association was called *The Hindi Association of the Pacific Coast* with its own weekly paper *Ghadar*, as a tribute to the first freedom struggle in India in 1857. The head office, *Yugantar Ashram* ("Advent to a New Era Society"), was based in San Francisco. Based on *Ghadar's* revolutionary appeals, the association was later renamed the *Hindustan Ghadar Party*. Here is a glimpse of the appeal published in *Ghadar's* very first issue:

WANTED: Brave Soldiers to stir up Ghadar in India
PAY: Death
PRIZE: Martyrdom
PENSION: Liberty
FIELD OF BATTLE: India

Within two years of his arrival, Har Dayal had successfully made an impact on the Indian Americans who were all united under the umbrella of the Ghadar Party. His success, however, was short-lived as the British colluded with the American secret agents who infiltrated the Ghadar Party, using an informer called P.H.E. Pandian. Pandian submitted evidence against Har Dayal to indict him as an anarchist. He was arrested in 1914 in San Francisco. Within a couple of days of his release on bail, he fled to Switzerland with the help of his Irish and American supporters. During this intense, albeit brief, period, Har Dayal and his Ghadar Party accomplished the mission of spreading awareness of the Indian freedom struggle widely. The Party grew in size and opened offices in Canada, China, the Philippines, and other Far Eastern countries.

In 1914, the ship, the *Komagata Maru* with 376 passengers (mostly Indian laborers) was refused entry by the Canadian immigration authorities after two months of agitation and legal battle. The British authorities treated Indians with indifference and intolerance during the entire series of events related to this ship. After their return, these laborers helped stir up revolutionary zeal among Indians against the British. Meanwhile, in North America, in Har Dayal's absence, his heir Ram Chandra tried to continue the work of the Ghadar Party. However, differences of opinion developed between Bhagwan Singh and other Sikhs associated with Khalsa Diwan and Chandra, who was forced to resign. Chandra set up a new newspaper separately, and Singh captured the old party. Some role was played by the British authorities in this rift between the Indian revolutionaries, who were receiving some support from the Germans who wanted to weaken the British Empire.[9]

From 1915 to 1917, the British authorities continued to ask the United States to arrest the Indian freedom fighters in America. However, the U.S. Department of Justice kept turning down such demands, stating that US laws cannot prevent Indians from their struggle against the British Raj. In 1917, when the USA joined World War I, it became legally easier to charge the Indians with conspiring to aid the German enemy (Jensen 1988). As is now widely known, Bhagat Singh Thind, a Sikh Indian was denied American citizenship by the Supreme Court even though he had served in the US military during the war.[10] After several failed attempts by the British authorities, finally, the American authorities were convinced by the British after the USA entered World War I and they arrested the Ghadar leader Ram Chandra and seven of his colleagues, charging them with conspiring against Great Britain. This "Hindu-German Conspiracy Trial" was held in San Francisco from November 1917 to April 1918. It was a great success for the British authorities who succeeded, after four years, in crushing the Indian revolutionaries in the USA. The trial, however, came to a sudden end when Ram Chandra was assassinated by Ram Singh, a member of the rival Bhagwan Singh's group, as Chandra was suspected of being a British agent. Despite this tragic event, the majority of the American public were sympathetic to the Indian freedom struggle. Even the rumor that these Indian patriots were going to be deported resulted in a large number of protests against the U.S. Department of Justice. After this trial, American opinion remained against the British Raj as they agreed with the writings of Annie Besant and Lala Lajpat Rai (Gower n.d.). These post-Ghadar leaders gained even fuller recognition. For instance, Lajpat Rai wrote a feature article in *The New York Times* in which he argued for self-government for India, by invoking the American ideals. In his words,

> India had always stood for freedom of opinion, freedom of belief, and freedom of action but Britain had denied India "liberty of the press," the ability to determine its fiscal policies, and even the right to bear arms. It was now time for India to take its rightful place on the world political stage as a moral force of great magnitude.
>
> (ibid.)

Rai also met W. E. B. Du Bois, during his trip (Slate 2019, 110).

Karla Gower (n.d.) wrote her Master's thesis in the early 1990s at Arizona State University, on Agnes Smedley, an American woman journalist. According to Gower (1996), Smedley became involved with radicals in the USA, notably Margaret Sanger and Emma Goldman. Through Goldman, Smedley became aware of socialism and the Indian Nationalist Movement. In 1917, she met Lala Lajpat Rai, an Indian nationalist leader, living in New York, and joined the movement. She was charged under the Espionage Act for working to overthrow the British Raj. Later she became the secretary for an organization called *Friends of Freedom for India*. Agnes' papers, including letters she wrote on behalf of the Friends of Freedom for India, are in the library archives of Arizona State University. According to Gower, both *The New York Times* and the *San Francisco Chronicle* played a crucial role in forming a favorable public opinion in support of the Indian revolutionaries.

Conclusion: acceptance and rejection of Indian immigrants

From their earliest immigration to North America, Indians have had a che-quered past of acceptance and rejection within American society. In 1924, the year the Statue of Liberty was declared a national monument, a permanent quota-based immigration law was passed (Mehta 1998). The Statue welcomed everybody from all over the world with these great words of Emma Lazarus's famous 1883 sonnet 'The New Colossus,' "Give me your tired, your poor, your huddled masses yearning to breathe free."[11] However, the new immigration law passed in the same year proved to be a significant obstacle for all potential immigrants who were not from Western Europe. The American immigration gates were reopened only after 1965, thereby severely keeping the numbers of Asian immigrants much lower than those of the Western hemisphere immi-grants. Although in 1910, 1913, 1919, and 1920, Asian Indians were accep-ted as "Whites" by different US courts, in 1909, 1917, other courts and in 1923, even the Supreme Court classed South Asians as nonWhites, "an alienating and barbaric social and religious system, one that rendered 'Hindus' utterly unfit for membership in the 'civilization of the White men'" (Snow 2004, p. 268, cited in Joshi and Adams 2007). This categorization led to many Indians losing their American citizenship. Bhicaji Balsara is noted as an exception by Nico Slate (2019, 20), being a Parsi Indian, he was dis-tinguished from Hindu Americans and was treated as equal to White Americans and was granted American citizenship.

As mentioned earlier, in 1870, only 586 people who had been born in India were in the USA, and by 1900, this number stood at 2,031. In the 1910 census, the numbers had increased to 2,545 then but dropped to 2,406 by the 1940 census. Meanwhile, in comparison, on the other side of the globe, 200,000 Americans served in India during World War II (Slate 2019, 154). The next three American censuses had no category to identify Indian Americans, perhaps due to their meager numbers. However, in the 1980 Census, the group "Asian Indian" was reinstated, and, as of 2019, this includes people born in India, born in America, born in another country, and people of mixed race, for whom at least one parent is an "Asian Indian" (Chakravorty et al. 2017). Rajani Das (1923) wrote one of the ear-liest reports detailing the issues and conditions of Indian Americans in California and British Columbia. In 1946, President Truman signed another law granting a citizenship quota to 100 Indians annually. By 1965, their number had risen to 50,000.

After 1965, when the immigration system once again allowed Asians to come to the United States, two important channels through which Indians entered and made an impact in the United States were as doctors and musicians. In the next couple of chapters, we will survey the history and current status of both these phenomena. In Chapter 5, we will also look at Jain Americans, another minority community within the Indian American community.

Notes

1 See https://religionnews.com/2019/01/27/tulsi-gabbards-2020-bid-raises-questions-about-hindu-political-ties/ (accessed May 13, 2019).
2 See www.pbs.org/wnet/religionandethics/2009/04/24/april-24-2009-ancient-christians-in-india/2754/ (accessed May 13, 2019).
3 See https://timesofindia.indiatimes.com/city/hyderabad/Mosque-in-Kerala-dates-back-to-the-Prophets-time/articleshow/48138989.cms (accessed May 13, 2019).
4 See http://diGītālhistories.yctl.org/2014/11/01/elihu-yale-was-a-slave-trader/ (accessed May 13, 2019).
5 See www.pem.org/about-pem/museum-history (accessed May 13, 2019).
6 See https://archive.org/details/comparisonofinst00prie/page/n4 (accessed May 13, 2019).
7 Emerson, Ralph W, and Merton M. Sealts. *The Journals and Miscellaneous Notebooks of Ralph Waldo Emerson*: Vol. 10 (Cambridge, MA: Belknap Press of Harvard University Press, 1973).
8 See www.facebook.com/pg/Guyana-Hindu-Dharmic-Sabha-175973365839875 (accessed July 10, 2017).
9 Gower, Karla K., "The Hindu-German Conspiracy: An Examination of the Framing of Indian Nationalists in Newspapers from 1915–1918." Available at: https://list.msu.edu/cgi-bin/wa?A3=ind9709d&L=AEJMC&E=7BIT&P=3267393&B=–&T=TEXT%2FPLAIN;%20charset=US-ASCII (accessed May 4, 2019).
10 See https://supreme.justia.com/cases/federal/us/261/204/ (accessed May 13, 2019).
11 See www.theatlantic.com/entertainment/archive/2018/01/the-story-behind-the-poem-on-the-statue-of-liberty/550553/ (accessed May 13, 2019).

3 Indians and Ayurveda in the American food and healthcare industries

Introduction

Although Deepak Chopra,[1] Sanjay Gupta,[2] Atul Gawande,[3] and Vivek Murthy[4] currently are some of the best-known Indian doctors in the USA, Indian doctors have come a long way in their struggle for equal recognition, starting in the second half of the twentieth century. In his memoir, Ved Mehta (1998, cited in Kumar 2004) recalls his first entry to the United States in August of 1949 when an American immigration officer disparaged Indian doctors "as a breed known to be susceptible to string-pulling, blandishments, and bribery." Another highly accomplished physician of Indian origin, Abraham Verghese in his *New Yorker* articles, as cited in ibid., shared a similar comment from one of his friends, who remarked in the early 1980s, "We are, my dear friend, like a transplanted organ—lifesaving, and desperately needed, but rejected because we are foreign tissue." Regardless of this aversion to Indian and other foreign medical graduates (FMGs), Indian doctors have harbored the American dream for decades, and the image of Indian doctors has dramatically improved in recent years. In addition to Indian doctors, the chapter also delves into the reception and flourishing of Ayurveda, the traditional Indic healthcare system, in America, by taking a closer look at several Ayurvedic pioneers and doctors. The chapter ends with some discussion on how Indian culinary ideas continue to survive and thrive in America.

Arrival and survival of Indian doctors from the 1960s onwards

Indian doctors started coming to North America in the mid-1960s. Many came on one-year Exchange Visitor Visas that were granted, based on acceptance as a trainee (intern/resident) in one of the accredited hospitals, of which there were many in several states, with California and some other states being exceptions. Many initially thought of learning advanced medicine for a few years and returning home to India. Since the American degrees, known as Board Certification did not carry significant value in India then, many Indian doctors had to consider doing further studies, such as becoming an MRCP (Member of the Royal College of Physicians) or an FRCS (Fellow of the Royal College of Surgeons) in the UK or Canada to fortify their résumés to get a better position on returning to India.

The first Indian doctors had to survive on meager salaries, and do all sorts of menial jobs, such as maintaining equipment or drawing blood for tests, that specified ancillary staff perform these days. Indian doctors used to remain on call, often on alternate nights and weekends stretching from Fridays to Mondays (currently the hours are regulated by law). Medical training was rewarding, but in return, Indian doctors provided the "cheap labor" essential to keep medical facilities functioning. Those who wanted to stay longer had to keep on going for additional training, a prerequisite for the renewal of visas on an annual basis.

In 1972, the immigration laws were changed, and foreign physicians were allowed to become immigrants. The new immigration system opened the floodgates for doctors from all around the world, the majority from India. Everyone still needed the ECFMG (Educational Council for Foreign Medical Graduates) certification – the last such one-day examination, which also tested English language skills. This examination was offered in India in the 1960s. The aspirants then started traveling to Colombo, Malaysia, and Pakistan to obtain this crucial credential.

At around the same time, foreign doctors became eligible to take the FLEX (Federal Licensing Examination) in most states, although California and a few other states still did not open it to FMGs (Foreign Medical Graduates). And now, with a license to practice and often with "board certification," the status of FMGs changed to teaching faculty, practitioners/attending physicians, and even specialists, with provision for hospital admitting privileges (although the elite facilities still barred them for one reason or another, mostly by inserting special requirements that were difficult to fulfill). The last planeloads of such new immigrant doctors arrived on December 31, 1976, and then the doors were slammed shut – for a little while. This influx resulted in overcrowding and decreasing opportunities for this new crop that reached a crisis stage in the late 1970s. Even some brilliant Indian medical graduates could not land a training position.

During that time, with the proliferation of private medical schools in countries such as Mexico, Trinidad, India, Hungary, and Poland that offered admission to those who were able to pay the capitation fees, the number of American positions given to FMGs kept shrinking. And since many of these non-American schools were able to affiliate with mainland American institutions for clinical work, their graduates often were given preference over other FMGs who lacked such affiliations.

Over the years, the ECFMG was replaced by a visa-qualifying examination that evolved into a three-part series: the United States Medical Licensing Examination (USMLE), with its final part to be completed in the USA, with visa options being H1B or J1. With the competition so fierce, many Indian physicians had to take research positions or enroll for additional degrees, such as Masters in Public Health, that helped them to get the reference letters. And after training, most were required to serve in rural areas before they could apply for an immigrant visa. A more accessible alternative, for a few select ones, has been a teaching faculty position in a medical school at a lower pay where eventually they obtain their Green Card to stay in America.

Organizing the physicians of Indian origin

As of 2019, the situation has changed considerably. Now, Indian doctors in America are well organized with the help of AAPI (the American Association of Physicians of Indian Origin), the largest ethnic organization with more than 100,000 physicians (Bhalla 2010). AAPI was founded in 1982 and has more than 150 chapters, alumni associations, and specialty societies. One of the critical co-founders of AAPI, Navin Shah, has described AAPI's genesis in several articles and news reports that he shared with me during his trip to Dallas in October 2017. In his June 19, 2004 article in AAPI's newsletter, he recollects that, in 1980, as president of the Indian Medical Association of America in Washington, DC, he set the ball rolling to form a national association of physicians of Indian origin. He contacted various smaller similar organizations individually and also published similar appeals in prominent Indian newspapers. After his discussions with the Detroit-based leaders, the first convention took place there in 1982 and AAPI was launched with Ujamal Kothari as the founding president and Navin Shah as the founding vice-president and later as the second president. With around 20 percent of graduating medical students in the USA of Indian origin, AAPI membership numbers continue to grow. The number of children of Indian immigrants graduating from US medical students is steadily increasing, soon estimated to reach 20 percent of the classes. In several hospitals in California, New York, New Jersey, and elsewhere in the country, every third or fourth doctor is of Indian origin (other Asian American doctors are also found in good numbers). Many prestigious institutions such as the Mayo Clinic, the Cleveland Clinic, Brigham, Massachusetts General Hospitals of Harvard, Mount Sinai of New York, Cedars Sinai of Los Angeles that once were dominated by "White" physicians, now have Indian Americans in top leadership positions.

Fortunately, I had the opportunity to interview Navin Shah, one of the co-founders of AAPI. Here is what he told me. In 1967, during the Vietnam War, the United States of American needed a large number of doctors urgently. Instead of waiting for ten years, the average time needed for a doctor's training; President Lyndon B. Johnson signed a new law that facilitated the influx of foreign doctors. Thousands of foreign doctors came from as many as 110 different countries, with the vast majority being Indian. Most of the Indian and other foreign doctors were appointed in the rural areas of America, not preferred by White doctors. Most foreign doctors had to choose less lucrative specialties such as family practitioners, psychiatrists, or other specialties, while surgery and other more lucrative specialties went to White doctors. Back in the 1980s, there were about 20,000–70,000 foreign doctors who used to face different kinds of discrimination in areas such as residency positions, jobs, promotions, hospital privileges, licensing, reciprocities, issuance of malpractice insurance, and other areas of medical practice. Although a study proved their high competency and training, their merit was not sufficient for them to be treated with the same respect as US medical graduates.[5] When some of the Indian doctors approached the American Medical Association (AMA) about such issues, they didn't receive a proper response. In 1985, the Alliance of Foreign Medical Graduates was formed to unite all the foreign-born physicians that account for almost 25 percent of all physicians in the country. According to a 2010 list of international physicians, shared by Shah, about 48,000 physicians were from India out of the total 240,000 international physicians, and 950,000 total number of physicians in America.

Eventually, Shah and other international doctors decided to invest in hiring a lobbyist who helped them approach the US Senators in Washington, DC. Five Bills were introduced in Congress, including AS 1868-Sen Moynihan, HR 3773-Rep Solarz, and HR 3241-Rep Bates. These Bills had provisions to penalize states and institutions that practiced discrimination against international physicians. Shah and others testified several times in the process to present dozens of cases of discrimination although the AMA opposed these Bills. One of the laws helped bring a substantial change: to rename Foreign Medical Graduates as International Medical Graduates. This change helped doctors of 120 different countries who were no longer going to remain "foreign" forever after this change in terminology. With the congressional support given to international medical practitioners, the AMA finally agreed to create a new office in 1989 to cater to their needs. In 1992, President George H. W. Bush signed the law to support their cause. The Bill had several provisions, such as a central repository for International Medical Graduates (IMG) credentials, cancelation of federal funding for the residency programs that discriminated against IMGs, a national advisory council to make the licensure process fair, and a study by the U.S. Department of Health and Human Services (HHS) in ten states to check for any discrimination against IMGs. Since 1992, all IMGs have been offered the same examinations as US-born medical graduates.

Shah also met Mrs. Indira Gandhi and several other future Prime Ministers of India to discuss ways to improve healthcare back in India. They introduced 30 hours of medical education for doctors periodically instead of the lifelong certificate that did not need such renewed training earlier. A new medical education director was appointed in the USA, who was sent from India. Shah and his colleagues shared more modern technologies with the Indian doctors. Also, over 100 pieces of major medical equipment, including CT scan, dialysis machines, x-ray units, mammography, operating microscopes, etc. were donated to Indian government hospitals. Also, AAPI annual events invite Indian artists to promote Indian art and culture. Indian American doctors have conducted hundreds of seminars and courses in more than 20 specialties in different institutions across India. Thousands of Indian physicians have benefitted from them. Several Indian charity dispensaries have also been funded.

Today, out of about 950,000 doctors in the USA, about 70,000 are Indian Americans. There are about 15,000 doctors in training and approximately 120,000 who are medical students. About 10 percent of students and 10 percent of faculty are of Indian origin. Indian Americans lead several specialty organizations, such as the Association of Urologists.[6] As of 2019, AAPI represented 41,235 physicians and 12,000 medical students, fellows, and residents of Indian origin (Mishra 2016).

Ayurveda: the American way

In addition to the above brief history of Indian doctors in the United States, Indic ideas have made a significant impact on American consciousness through yoga, Ayurveda, and other healthcare practices. These are often included in the category of Complementary and Alternative Medicine (CAM), as shown by various contributors to the volume co-edited by Dagmar Wujastyk and Frederick M. Smith (Wujastyk and Smith 2008). Observers in that volume and elsewhere, such as Goldberg (2010), have noted the significant contributions by Maharishi Mahesh Yogi, Deepak Chopra, Robert Svoboda, Vasant Lad, David Frawley, Georg Feuerstein, Maya Tiwari, Atreya Smith, and other pioneers. Most of them continue to travel and promote Ayurveda and related Indian cultural ideas widely. Organizations that continue to encourage Ayurveda include the National Ayurvedic Medical Association (NAMA), the Association of Ayurvedic Professionals of North America (AAPNA), the Council for Ayurveda Credentialing (CAC), the Kripalu School of Ayurveda (KSA), the American Institute of Vedic Studies (AIVS), the Ayurvedic Institute (AI), the Wise Earth Monastery (WEM), Vinayak Panchakarma (VP), the California College of Ayurveda (CCA), and the American University of Complementary Medicine (AUCM). With such a plethora of perspectives and approaches for practicing Ayurveda, students are exposed to a wide variety at each of these organizations. Some of them carry the imprints of their founders, such as David Frawley at AIVS, Marc Halpern at CCA, Swamini Mayatitananda at WEM, Sunil Joshi at VP, Parla Jayagopal at AUCM, and Vasant Lad at AI. Many of them continue to be the leading teachers at their respective institutions where they are regarded by their students as spiritual gurus as well. Most institutions have evolved into lineage-based systems where they hire their graduates predominantly. In some cases, such practices have also led to rivalries among them (Welch 2008, 133).

Sita Reddy wrote her PhD dissertation on "The Reinvention of Ayurvedic Medicine in New Age America." In her (2002) article, Reddy argues that Ayurveda in America is heavily influenced by American medical culture as well as the religious culture of America. The New Age interests in alternative lifestyles have significantly contributed to the growing interest in Ayurveda. This "New Age" connection seems to be similar to the acceptance of Indian classical music in the 1960s by jazz and pop musicians who were also exploring non-Western musical cultures. Similar to the musical collaborations,

Ayurveda has also evolved into multiple forms, genres, and lineages established by pioneers such as Maharishi Mahesh Yogi and Vasant Lad, among others. American Ayurveda has emerged

> as a uniquely Indian ethnomedicine, in the form of a cultural commodity for primarily non-Indian audiences. It can be summarized as a New Age healing system that conflates science, religion, and ancient tradition. Ayurveda is portrayed in media in three different ways: as a system of vegetarianism and dietary discipline, as a system of rejuvenation, and as a system of ascetic health and well-being. While the first is about purification, the second [is] about replenishment and [the] third about personal transformation.
>
> (ibid.)

In her (2011) article, Maya Warrier provides a useful survey of Ayurveda in the Western context. She notes that Ayurveda globally competes against much more powerful and "well-established biomedical pharmaceutical industry supported by the governmental forces, over resources, markets and knowledge systems."

According to Svoboda (2008, 122), compared to Chinese medicine, Ayurveda has had less success in the United States for several reasons. First, less acceptance and appreciation of Ayurveda by Indian Americans. Second, the Indian government's support for Ayurveda is merely symbolic. Third, the sharp differences and divisions among Indian Ayurvedic practitioners in India. Svoboda estimated that about 200 BAMS (Bachelor of Ayurvedic, Medicine and Surgery) Ayurvedic doctors are in the UK compared to about 30 such doctors in the USA, in the early twenty-first century. However, as of 2019, according to some practicing Ayurvedic doctors that I interviewed, the numbers of BAMS doctors in North America has reached over 600, although not all of them are practicing. Svoboda expressed his concerns that, like yoga, Ayurveda is bound to be exploited for commercial profit. As the first non-Indian BAMS Ayurvedic doctor, he endorsed the accreditation procedure that some organizations are trying to institutionalize in the USA, albeit with the caveat that the process should establish the highest standards rather than diluting them to accommodate the less trained practitioners. Many practitioners with degrees or diplomas in Chinese medicine, massage therapy, chiropractic practice, and naturopathy, often add Ayurveda as an additional practice in their portfolio without much in-depth study of Ayurveda in many cases (Welch 2008, 137). Perhaps the most prominent example of this is Deepak Chopra, who connects the three Ayurvedic *doshas* to the control of movement, metabolism, digestion, physical structure, and fluid balance (Saks 2008, 37). According to Mike Saks (ibid., 29), the White House Commission on Complementary and Alternative Medicines in 2002, paved the way for better acceptance and promotion of Ayurveda among other similar CAM systems. Saks (ibid., 32) cited a 1998 report to note that about two-fifths of

American population annually consult some CAM practitioners. In 2002, California's alternative healthcare law started providing legal protection for practitioners of alternative healthcare, including Ayurveda.

Exploring Ayurveda in Texas and beyond

As I began looking for Ayurvedic doctors and practitioners, I came across five names in the Dallas area, Texas, where I live. Out of the five,[7] four have Ayurvedic degrees from India but do not have a license to practice Ayurveda in the USA. One has degrees in Food and Nutrition and is actively promoting Ayurvedic ideas about food and nutrition with her focus on veganism and vegetarianism. Two are working at the Ayurveda centers in Coppell, a suburb of Dallas Fort Worth Metroplex. Below are some of the excerpts from my interviews with them.

As a resident of Coppell, I was pleasantly surprised to see the new sign for "Santhigram Wellness Kerala Ayurveda Center" in one of the strip malls here in the North Texas area.[8] A beautifully decorated front desk with a Hindu image in the background and the fragrance of incense sticks welcomed me as I entered the center. Soon, Sangeetha Sridharan, the owner, and manager of this center emerged from her office, and we began talking. It was her family health issues that inspired her to launch this new Ayurvedic center in the Dallas area in 2016. She told me how she, with support from her husband, worked tirelessly to design this center, and hired an Ayurvedic doctor, Amba Prabhakar, from India. Her center was inaugurated by the Mayor of Irving on Saturday, July 9, 2016, in a leased store. The center is just one of the several locations of the network of such Ayurvedic centers across the USA. As of 2019, they have 11 centers across the USA, including 4 in New Jersey, 3 in New York, 2 in Texas, 1 in Illinois, and 1 in Wisconsin. This Santhigram Ayurvedic network is co-led by Gopinathan Nair and his wife Ambika Nair, an Ayurvedic doctor by training, and they opened their first center in New Jersey in 2008 (Nair 2017).

The Ayurvedic doctor at this Santhigram center in Coppell is Amba Prabhakar who is on L1 intracompany transferee non-immigrant visa. In an interview, she told me her story:

> I obtained my Ayurveda degree from the Government Medical College in Bangalore and then practiced Ayurveda in Kerala, Karnataka, New Delhi, and Geneva, before moving to Dallas in 2016. American patients who visit our Santhigram Center in Coppell are pretty aware and interested in Ayurveda, in some cases, even more, knowledgeable than their Indian counterparts. They choose Ayurveda because they have not received permanent remedies from the Western medical system. They like and enjoy the holistic system of the chemical-free, nature-based system of Ayurveda and expect to resolve the root causes of their health issues. Patients of chronic diseases prefer Ayurveda, e.g., infertility issues, menstrual issues, or arthritis. Some of

my patients have now completely stopped going to their PCP (Primary Care Physician) and depend solely on Ayurveda. They visit their PCP only when I force them to do so! Our Ayurvedic fees are comparable to the copays and premiums people pay to visit their PCP, so we are pretty affordable. We have several treatments for maintaining good health, e.g., to maintain good eyesight, to maintain proper blood pressure, thyroid, and sugar levels, etc. However, Ayurvedic treatments are like daily regimented exercises. They involve lifestyle changes and work only with proper discipline. Many PCPs refer their patients to physical therapists. Ayurvedic therapies can similarly be referred to by the PCPs for even more benefits, and hopefully, American insurance companies will cover them too in future. Ayurvedic doctors are forced to learn about Western medicines, so it should be vice versa too. Ayurveda has a bright future, especially in gynecological and geriatrics issues. All the eight branches of Ayurveda are not yet developed in America: *Vrishya Chikitsa* (rejuvenation), *Damstra Chikitsa* (toxicology), *Jara Chikitsa* (geriatrics), *Bhoot Chikitsa* (psychiatry), *Shalya Chikitsa* (surgery), *Kaya Chikitsa* (internal medicine), *Bala Chikitsa* (pediatrics), and *Urdhvanga Chikitsa* (treatment of eyes, ears, nose, throat, and head). We can practice almost all of these in America as there are now several Ayurvedic doctors here. However, getting some of the authentic medicines is a bit difficult due to customs issues. Also, we avoid using lead or mercury in any of our treatment as those need extra precaution in handling. We also avoid certain therapies that involve bloodletting. However, some of the herbs that are available in America are better than those available in India! Most of the Indian companies sell so-called Ayurvedic medicines in which authentic Ayurvedic herbs are present only for the namesake, so their effect on our health is also insufficient. Quackery and improper use of Ayurvedic labeling have to be stopped in India too to maintain the good reputation of authentic Ayurvedic therapies. We also need to promote more herbal gardens to grow more Ayurvedic herbs. We have to make Ayurveda "cool" for youngsters. Also, Ayurvedic doctors in the United States, unlike in India, should be prepared to provide therapies such as massages. We have been privileged to help some Muslim families who had fertility issues. With our treatment, when children were born in their family, they invited us to Irving Mosque where we shared about our services. Our mission is to make people happy, to care for them, and to help alleviate their suffering. Many of our American patients prefer only Indian therapists for Ayurveda, just as at a Chinese restaurant, they prefer Chinese chefs.

I met another Ayurvedic doctor, Dhanada Kulkarni, and learned some interesting details about the journey of Ayurveda in North America. She reminded me that Ayurveda is intertwined with yoga and other Hindu ideas that Swami Vivekananda first brought to America in 1893. After many more gurus in the next century, it was finally Maharishi Mahesh Yogi who emphasized and promoted Ayurveda in an organized manner in the mid-1980s with the establishment of the Maharishi Ayurveda Association of America, affiliated with the Maharishi Transcendental Meditation organization. Others also contributed in their ways to bring Ayurveda to America, such as Vinod Seth, who founded the South Western Ayurvedic Center in 1986, Swami Krishnananda, who started the Ayurvedic Holistic Center, and Ted Warren, who started the National Center for Ayurvedic Medicine. Since the beginning, it has maintained tangible or intangible links with religion that obviated the need for any professional accreditation. Much Ayurvedic practice and education still occur in this way with just a couple of exceptions, such as in California where the state approved an educational program. With the lack of any government approval, most of the Ayurvedic practices tend to focus on maintaining good health with massage and different kinds of cleansing and healing treatments rather than curing a disease with herbs. Ayurvedic doctors also tend to emphasize the holistic aspects of their treatment that takes into account the social and environmental issues of the patient and try to cure the entire physical, mental, and spiritual being of a patient. Maharishi invited many Ayurvedic scholars from India who collaborated with Western doctors to promote Ayurveda as an integrated health system. Deepak Chopra was an early disciple of Maharishi in the 1980s. Cynthia Ann Humes recalls:

> Chopra began to study with Maharishi's head Ayurveda specialist, Brihaspati Dev Triguna. Subsequently, Chopra established the Maharishi Vedic Health Center in Lancaster, Massachusetts. Chopra possessed an unusual ability to explain complex Ayurveda teachings in simple language, providing great exposure and credibility to Maharishi's medical programs. Chopra was elevated first to the presidency of the newly minted American Association of Ayur-Vedic Medicine. Shortly after that, Maharishi referred to him publicly as "Dhanvantari of Heaven on Earth," a richly symbolic title, evocative of Vedic mythology's Dhanvantari: the physician to the gods themselves ... Chopra eventually broke off from Maharishi and launched his venture. By providing more accessible explanations, he remains an industry leader, offering an array of alternatives competing both with his former rishi as well as with the Western medical establishment for consumer health dollars.
>
> (2008, 323)

According to Kulkarni, Ayurveda is like riding a bike. It works at a slow speed and involves fewer risks compared to driving a car. It can cure the deadliest diseases, such as AIDS, cancer, diabetes, heart diseases, and thyroid problems, but requires time and a balanced lifestyle. Kulkarni founded her Ayurvedic institute in the Dallas area in 2006 and her Ayurveda Center in Coppell in 2019. She earned her Bachelor's degree in Ayurvedic Studies from Kavi Kalidas University in Aurangabad and was the Gold Medalist in her state of Maharashtra. She also completed her Master's degree from Kolkata and Acharya course from Yoga University, Nashik. Since her arrival in the

USA, Kulkarni has received several diplomas in massage therapy, and integrated board medicine, reiki, *prāṇa* (life force) healer, and in *vāstu śāstra* (the Indic system of architecture). She started her career at a holistic health center in Greenville, South Carolina, in 2005 and worked in other states before settling in Texas. Unlike many Ayurvedic students in India, she deliberately rejected an allopathic medical career after a paralytic attack when she was merely 19 years of age because of her recovery with the help of Ayurvedic treatment from that attack. Her mother is a Vedic astrologer and also works as an administrator with local colleges in Maharashtra, India. She regards Prabhakar Tanaji Joshi, who runs the Prabha Ayurveda Foundation in Maharashtra, as her guru.[9] The foundation has provided Ayurvedic knowledge and care to many students and patients for free. Kulkarni recalled that Joshi had successfully cured a patient who had uterine cancer even though she had been declared incurable by allopathic doctors. Kulkarni shared that she had successfully cured the insomnia of a Russian American piano teacher. Kulkarni is also associated with the Council for Ayurveda Credentialing (CAC) that has met regularly, since 2011, to develop the lesson plans for the standardization of the curriculum of Ayurveda in the USA. CAC has also developed open-source documents to improve the understanding of Ayurvedic education in the USA. As of 2019, there are about 55 Ayurvedic institutes in North America. Kulkarni counted Shekhar Annambhotla, Shunya Pratichi Mathur, and Suhas Khirsagar as other prominent contemporary Ayurvedic practitioners in the USA.

Another Ayurvedic doctor that I interviewed in the Dallas area was Gauri Junnarkar Chaudhuri. According to Chaudhuri, most Americans who choose Ayurveda consider it "the sister science" of yoga and come to Ayurveda as the next step in their journey towards well-being. Shekhar Annambhotla, another Ayurvedic doctor in Pennsylvania and an ex-student of Maharishi Mahesh Yogi, added that people dissatisfied with allopathy, many Indian Americans, and other holistic health practitioners choose Ayurveda. According to Chaudhuri, some aspects from Ayurveda, such as its dietary habits, use of spices, and Ayurvedic herbs with holistic nutrition can be promoted in America. Ayurvedic therapies such as yoga, meditation, massages, *Shirodhara* (head massage therapy), *Swedan* (steam bath), *Kati-Basti* (therapy for lower back), and the overall nature-based lifestyle can be promoted for stress management. When she came to the Dallas area in 2002, Ayurveda was still a very new phenomenon. She obtained her Master of Science in Nutrition from Texas Woman's University, became a licensed dietitian, and worked in the hospital system in Outpatient Diabetes for several years. She went back to school and became a licensed massage therapist as well and started integrating Ayurvedic therapies with her training in nutrition and massage therapy, calling it *Ayurnutrition*. She hoped that one day, Ayurveda would be accredited and combined with the mainstream American healthcare system.

The roots of American Ayurveda: Vasant Lad, the pioneer

One of the Ayurvedic pioneers, Vasant Lad, came to the USA in 1979 at the invitation of Lenny Blank, an alternative medicine entrepreneur in Santa Fe, New Mexico (Svoboda 2008, 121). Lad established the Ayurvedic Institute in Albuquerque in New Mexico in 1984 and emphasized teaching more than a clinical practice that continues to suffer from lack of accreditation across North America. In June 2018, I visited Dr. Vasant Lad's Ayurvedic Institute in Albuquerque in New Mexico. Below are some excerpts from my interviews with his colleague, Wynn Werner.

> A student of Dr. Lad many years ago told me that in many ways, it is unfortunate that Dr. Lad was our very first Ayurvedic teacher. When we were so new to Ayurveda, and we were so young, we did not understand the differences between Dr. Lad, the vaidya, the person who has the significant amount of clinical experience and Dr. Lad, the man, who also has a long spiritual practice. Why is that? Is that because of our lack of understanding of Ayurveda or our lack of spiritual practice or our Western cultural values getting in the way of our understanding of the integration of the body, the mind, and the soul? Only later as we have grown older and have more understanding of others' contributions, we have been able to appreciate each of those components so that we can work on them ourselves and also those skills of Dr. Lad's that he is so humble. When we attempt to take a pulse, we most likely have a shallow understanding compared to what Dr. Lad does. Which part is responsible for that lesser understanding? It is always the training, education, and experience, as Dr. Lad would say. However, from my long observation of this, I would venture to say that it is Dr. Lad's spiritual development that enables him to understand so much about a patient. We are more limited in our abilities in relating to our clients and students. It can perhaps not be proved scientifically by any measuring instrument or device. Why does each of us pick a particular teacher – a spiritual teacher or an academic teacher? Why do we pick a particular dentist, medical doctor, or surgeon? Generally speaking, it is not a scientific explanation that the Western world puts so much emphasis on. It ignores these holistic connections of body, mind, and spirit between the Ayurvedic practitioners and their students and patients. The more the Ayurvedic doctors are holistically and spiritually integrated in terms of their bodies, the minds, and the spirit, the better practitioners they will become. This integration determines their ability to be able to connect with another person at all the different levels and is in contrast to Western medicine that is heading towards vertical specialization without knowing the person at all levels. One goes to doctor A for the disease A and doctor B for disease B but who is tying it all together? The patients are left to do that themselves, and they are often not well prepared for such integration. When we have

a holistic perspective, we can focus on the removal of the cause of disease in the integrated system of the body, the mind, and the spirit, as a whole. The cause of the physical suffering may be spiritual, emotional, or *samskāras* (karmic consequences from previous lifetimes), which the Western medical science would never accept. Therefore, Dr. Lad includes *jyotiṣa śāstra* (Indic system of astrology) and *vāstu śāstra* (the Indic system of architecture) in his diagnoses. In his intuition, he often figures out that the cause of a disease can be from patients' ancestors or unresolved problems from the previous lifetimes. The symptoms could be fruits of the seeds of karma sown in previous lifetimes, as agreeable to the Indic spiritual traditions that accept reincarnation and karma theories. Griefs and sadness can manifest in disease related to the lungs, or anxiety can appear as a symptom in the colon, for instance. That is why many Westerners are now very interested in the spiritual aspects of traditional Chinese medicines and Ayurveda even as many practitioners in India and China are adopting more Western ways, ironically! In many cases, the Western seekers are going to China and India, in remote forests and mountains in many instances, to learn the ancient traditional practices whereas the governments of these countries are going the other ways! Even many Indian and Chinese patients now prefer a pill rather than to deal with the causes of their symptoms. They are not ready to transform their lifestyle to solve their health problems. Recent graduates of Ayurvedic medical degrees in India may well diagnose the causes of the diseases but often fail to convince their clients about transforming the lifestyles to remove the causes of various issues. Often patients prefer the "magic" pill or surgery instead. Maybe in ancient times, people dared to listen to the truth. People who are interested in the authentic Ayurvedic teaching come to Dr. Lad. Many people come from past careers in IT, finance, and engineering because they now seek a more spiritually fulfilling career. They give up the luxuries of those lucrative careers to become humble students of Ayurveda. About 20 to 40 people join in the 1st year program. About 10 to 20 people join in the 2nd year program. They take 21 hours per week in intensive courses with weekly quizzes in ten-week courses with homework, final projects, quarterly exams, and oral exams with Dr. Lad. We also offer weekend seminars that are attended by a few hundred students each year. Overall, we have trained more than 1,000 students in the last couple of decades since our inception.

At their center, I realized that Ayurveda is one of the few skills that can only be learned by becoming an apprentice, i.e., by living and learning in the presence of the teacher. In the Western world, many people want Ayurveda to be accepted as fair and included among other diverse health traditions. Ayurveda and other Indic traditions evolved differently in America as compared to Chinese medicine and other Chinese traditions. Ayurveda did not flourish in the Indian American communities, unlike Chinese medicine that continues to thrive in the Chinese communities. Ayurveda has instead grown because of the focused group of committed people who have worked hard for Ayurveda's success. American people depend on their government who grants a license and certification only to particular kind of doctors. People are not allowed to go to non-licensed practitioners. Because of this, Ayurveda cannot yet be widely practiced in America. New laws are being passed to protect unlicensed, traditional healthcare practitioners from charges of "practice of medicine without a license." Today, although nine American states, Oklahoma, Idaho, Minnesota, Rhode Island, California, Louisiana, New Mexico, Arizona, and Colorado have a Health Freedom Law to allow the unlicensed, traditional healthcare practitioners, licensing is still needed to protect the reputation of Ayurveda. Ayurvedic practitioners trained in India must be fully knowledgeable about the healthcare laws in America. As in other healthcare systems, Ayurvedic practitioners in America have also formed their associations, e.g., NAMA co-founded in 1998 by Wynn Werner, Kumar Batra, Cynthia Copple, and Marc Halpern. All four met monthly for a couple of years, and after intense discussions, finally, in 2000, NAMA was incorporated as a 501c6 organization in California. Its first conference was held in Austin, Texas, in 2003.

According to the NAMA website (www.AyurvedaNama.org), NAMA has 12 directors who are elected by more than 1,300 members who meet at its annual conference in different American cities. NAMA works with more than 30 different Ayurvedic schools spread across the country. Professional members can be counselors, practitioners, or doctors. Counselors are "trained in preventive healthcare as well as health-promotion with a specific focus on diet and lifestyle through traditional Ayurvedic medical science principles and practices." Practitioners are "trained in preventive healthcare, nutrition, lifestyle pathology, and disease management through traditional Ayurvedic medical science principles and practice." Doctors "use the same diagnostic tools and therapeutic methods as the practitioner, but with greater depth of knowledge and breadth of experience. The doctor has a much deeper understanding of history, classical texts, and pathology."

Wynn Werner reminded me of the recent documentary *The Doctor from India* (2018) on Dr. Lad. Dr. Lad has tried hard to preserve the Sanskrit terms of Ayurveda. For instance, as the Western medical system has etiology, Ayurveda has *Nidan*, and for pathology, Ayurveda has *Samprapti*. An Ayurvedic counselor is limited to learning the first few stages of diagnosis of a disease out of the six steps of *Samprapti*. But a practitioner can go further to diagnose in the next stages too, primarily, after the disease has already been named and identified. And, finally, a doctor is the ultimate expert, with much more clinical experience and also significant understanding to integrate Western medicines with Ayurveda. Werner further told me that in the last couple of decades, most Ayurvedic development has happened at smaller independent institutes in America outside of prominent universities. However, most of the research funding and government attention went to the universities even if they may not be promoting Ayurveda as much as smaller institutes. NAMA is trying to build bridges between government agencies and private Ayurvedic institutes. Below are Vasant Lad's responses to some of my other questions when I interviewed him in his office in Albuquerque, New Mexico, in June 2018.

PJ: What kind of people in America choose Ayurvedic treatment? Why do they do so? What are their expectations? How do they experience Ayurvedic treatment modalities, and how do they make sense of their experience?

DR. LAD: Ayurveda is an ancient medical and healing art with roots in Ṛig Veda and Atharva Veda. It came to America two decades ago, and, slowly, common people started loving the Ayurvedic principles. It is not just a medical science but is a science of living in harmony with nature. So that *Jeevet Sharada Shatam*, meaning let us live long for 100 years, the Vedic oath is based on Ayurveda. Ayurveda is slowly becoming popular. NAMA is working hard to bring Ayurveda to the mainstream. With various practitioners and doctors learning Ayurveda, it is taking roots in America. Modern Western medicine is a complete system with all kinds of technologies, specializations, surgeries, etc. It can deal with all kinds of diseases and emergencies, but it is missing something. It currently has no permanent remedy for chronic diseases such as for Parkinson's or arthritis. It is pretty good in treating the body and to some extent the mind; the spirit is out of the question. Ayurveda treats the whole person, including the body, the mind, the spirit. The modern medical system works statistically and quantitatively, but Ayurveda treats each person uniquely and qualitatively. Ayurveda treats ten patients with the same disease in ten different ways, unlike the modern Western medical system. People who are left uncured and unsatisfied eventually come to Ayurveda in search of a better and permanent solution. For thousands of years, Ayurveda has been saying that each person has a unique *Prakriti* (constitution) and also unique *Vikriti* (current state). There are hazardous side effects of Western medicines, and patients with such side effects often come to Ayurveda. Patients also come to Ayurveda for the medicine and philosophy that brings internal communication between body, mind, and consciousness. Ayurveda teaches how to listen to the body, mind, and spirit. Self-knowledge is the foundation of life. If you do not know yourself, what you are, all the other kind of knowledge, qualifications, and degrees have no value. Self-knowledge is the foundation of life, and this means knowing what my body type is, what is my psychological *Prakriti*, how my consciousness operates, and interactions of the three doshas, *Vāta, Pitta, Kapha*. These three principles of life govern our unique psycho-physiology and consciousness. People coming to Ayurveda have a lot of expectations. It is the responsibility of the Ayurvedic doctor to understand what those expectations are. Ayurveda teaches responsibility, and this kind of treatment is not a quick-fix. I am responsible for my suffering, insecurity, anger, frustration, depression. There is no magic pill here. We have to learn how one's response is to a situation.

How they make sense of the Ayurvedic experience. We at our Institute have all kinds of Ayurvedic treatments, including *Panchakarmā*, massage, and counseling. We advise proper diet, the art of thinking, lifestyle, yoga, and meditation. For instance, we had a hepatitis patient whose viral load came down drastically after treatment. Similarly, a patient of Parkinson's had tremors reduced by 75%.

PJ: What kind of people in America choose to study Ayurveda? How has this changed over time?

DR. LAD: These are very honest and sincere people who have studied their healing systems and have realized the limitations of Western medical science. These include chiropractors, acupuncturists, psychotherapists, yoga therapists, and modern medical doctors. Even Ayurveda has its limitations, as no medical system is a complete system. So, these people feel that they are looking for alternatives. For instance, the Western modern medical system is lacking the concepts of nutrition and prevention. Some people believe that vaccination has its hazardous side effects but is used for prevention. Also, many people come to learn Ayurveda for self-healing. That was the theme of my first book, *Ayurveda: The Science of Self-Healing*. Many healthcare practitioners come to learn Ayurveda to try to integrate its principles into their medical systems. Ayurveda is in need of time. Although it is an ancient Indian system, it is new in America and is the future of medicine. In my travels across North America, South America, Europe, and Asia, Ayurveda is becoming popular. Many healthcare practitioners look at Ayurveda as their new guru because, in it, there are basic principles of the modern Western medical system, acupuncture, homeopathy, etc. In this way, the ancient system of Ayurveda is the mother of all other healing systems. So, it is changing over time, and more and more people are becoming open to receiving Ayurveda.

PJ: Which of the traditional elements from Indian Ayurveda can be preserved and promoted in America?

DR. LAD: Ayurvedic practices are based on the six principles of Indian philosophy. Ayurveda is also based on the *Pancha Mahābhuta*, the five-element theory of space, air, water, fire, and earth. Students should learn these theories and principles. For instance, bones and hair represent the earth element, secretions represent water, respiration represents air, and metabolism represents fire. The body is made up of five elements. These Ayurvedic principles are universally applicable, including even for astronauts in outer space. Without these basics of Ayurveda, it cannot be practiced anywhere.

PJ: What is your view of the arrival of Ayurveda in America?

DR. LAD: When I came in the late 1970s, there was much less awareness about Ayurveda. I gave lectures at different universities, health centers, and yoga centers. I traveled a lot from the East to the West Coast, visiting different places to talk about Ayurveda. People were very open and welcoming. In this journey, people realized for the first time about the ideas of *Vāta*,

Pitta, Kapha, the basics of Ayurveda. Being a pure vegetarian, I had trouble finding the appropriate food, so I introduced *khichadi* in America. It is made of rice, lentils, turmeric, mustard, cumin seeds, and ghee. Perhaps the future of fast food is this wholesome dish which is cooked according to Ayurvedic principles.

PJ: What have been your contributions and vision for Ayurveda in America?

DR. LAD: Deepak Chopra, David Frawley, and many others have made contributions to Ayurveda in America. I was just privileged to be the first one to come and be able to teach Ayurveda. We are fortunate to be able to establish the Ayurvedic Institute in New Mexico. Insurance companies do not cover our services, but people pay out of pocket. Hopefully, in the future, some insurance companies will start covering Ayurvedic practices too. We need integrated hospitals and universities that provide and teach Ayurvedic practices also. Allopathic and Ayurvedic doctors will work together. Ayurveda is becoming popular across the world and has a good future everywhere.

PJ: Can Ayurveda be practiced in its original way in America?

DR. LAD: This will take time because, in the original system, several chemicals and metals including mercury, gold, silver, lead, and copper, are used that are not yet allowed in America. More research is required to test the toxicity of them, especially in the way they are used in Ayurveda. In India, mercury is being researched for its cancer-curing properties when used in a specific way.

Hopefully, these interviews with several Ayurvedic experts have given a wholesome and inclusive perspective on American Ayurveda. However, Ayurveda is not just about treating diseases but includes Indic cuisines and culinary ideas as well (Tuminello 2018). In the following section, we take a quick look at how these ideas are now widely available across America and what issues arise from such developments in North America.

Indian cuisines and culinary ideas in America

Indian cultural ideas are making some impact in America through the spread of Indian cuisine. In her pioneering book on Indian food studies, Anita Mannur (2010) shows that immigrant Indian existence is intertwined with their culinary practices. For instance, some Indian Americans prefer to describe their identity as a rotten coconut that is brown on the outside but black inside, while for others a coconut refers to being white inside, signifying their higher status in the American racialized class system. She goes on to examine how chicken tikka masala, although sometimes hailed as a dish symbolizing British multiculturalism, shows the consumption and commodification of racial identities and how race is imagined and reinterpreted within the cultural arena. She rhetorically asks what makes the Indian dish, chicken tikka masala, acceptable on British tables when the Indian people who made that dish are not welcome to share the table with the British. Also, she provides instances of the negative stereotypes of Indian food persistent in popular culture. Food, in some ways, also serves as a means for the sustenance of Indian identity and culture as well as nostalgia for the homeland.

Virendra Kalra (2004) focusses on the samosa, a traditional Indian food that has been adopted by many different cultures, including the British and American. His article highlights the various aspects of ethnic food in multiculturalism and argues that the samosa, like all traditional food, should be treated with respect, not only respect for the culture this food hails from but also respect for the people whom this food represents. Kalra laments that samosas are seen as a commodity, and its consumers ignore the fact that Indian women make these foods. Elizabeth Buettner (2008) makes a similar argument in her article.

Tulasi Srinivas (2006) discusses gastro-nostalgia associated with traditional Indian food. She explores the issue of diaspora women working full-time. One of the ways in which such women balance their family responsibilities with their professional life is by depending on packaged Indian food now widely available in Indian grocery stores across North America. Although these packs are sold as if they seem to mimic the traditional food, they help keep the connection with Indian heritage alive, especially for the Indian children born in North America.

Morgan et al. (2011) show that a variety of Indian food has been migrating around the world for the last few centuries. As of 2017, while America has become the most significant consumer and importer of spices, most of these spices are imported from countries such as India, according to a report on NPR (Hartke 2017). In 2015, the Epic Channel in India showed a series of small episodes lasting 5–10 minutes, highlighting different agricultural produce and minerals in which India has remained a dominant exporter for several millennia. The episodes that pertained to different agricultural produce were on black pepper, tea, chili, saffron, sesame, cumin, clove, fennel, cardamom, turmeric, cashew, cinnamon, coffee, and mustard. The Government of India's Indian Spices Board's website[10] shows that the USA remains the biggest importer from India of some of the items, such as pepper, celery, fennel, and oleoresin. It is also one of the top countries to import cardamom, chili, ginger, turmeric, coriander, cumin, fenugreek, nutmeg, garlic, curry powder, and mint.[11]

In addition to such imports, the USA has, of course, imported hundreds of thousands of Indians who consume some of these spices that are increasingly being imported into the USA. According to Josiam and Monteiro (2004), the children of Indian American restaurant owners, like most of other Indian immigrants, prefer science and technology-related careers and this is one of the reasons for the low numbers of Indian restaurants in the country. We can note this changing trend at one of the oldest Indian restaurants, Cosmic Café in Dallas.[12] This Indian restaurant was started in 1995 in the house of the late Kumar Pallana, who later moved to Hollywood and appeared in a few films. As of 2019, Praveen Sachdev manages the restaurant, and in addition to serving food, he also teaches meditation in Pallana's old bedroom there.

A 2015 report in the *Washington Post* (Ferdman 2015) was quoted by Krishnendu Ray, a food studies professor at New York University, and mentioned that there are about 5,000 Indian restaurants in the country compared to about 40,000 Chinese and 40,000 Mexican restaurants. According to Ray, New York City saw the number of Indian restaurants rising from 20 in the 1980s to more than 300 in 2015. Mannur (2010) mentions a 1921 article in *The New York Times* and a 1920 advertisement in *Young India* and confirms by citing Vivek Bald that the Taj Mahal Hindu Restaurant was one of the earliest Indian restaurants, established in 1918 in New York. Also, the Ceylon Restaurant was started in 1913, and the Ceylon India Inn was opened in 1923. Even earlier, Saint Nihal Singh wrote reports about Indian food in the *Chicago Daily Tribune*. As of 2015, in New York, although the numbers of Indian Americans are 20 times more than the numbers of Thai Americans, the number of Indian restaurants is almost the same as that of Thai restaurants. As of 2011, Indian food ingredients counted for about 1.2 percent of the total food sales. According to Ray, the slow and limited acceptance of Indian food is because of the higher cost and more intensive labor needed in its cooking. Although 2017 *Nation's Restaurants News* included Indian food as one of the significant new food trend (Johnson 2017), the 2019 National Restaurant Association did not have Indian food in any of its research reports.[13] The absence of Indian cuisine is in stark contrast to the near monopoly of Indian Americans in the other hospitality-related industry of owning and managing hotels and motels (Dhingra 2012).

Conclusion

In the last two decades at least, no American Presidential election has happened without debates and discussions about the American healthcare issues. While the costs of healthcare, prescription drugs, and insurance premiums continue to skyrocket, millions of Americans remain in the grip of crises such as the opioid epidemic, the obesity epidemic, various allergies, mental health issues, heart diseases, cancer, respiratory diseases, and many more.[14] Moreover, America continues to lack trained physicians and nurses, especially in emergency rooms and in rural areas.[15] Indian doctors and Indic healthcare ideas continue to contribute to both of these areas. Since the 1970s, Indian doctors have continued to arrive and serve American patients diligently, and Ayurvedic experts have also continued to visit and provide alternative healthcare to thousands of Americans. As America becomes more inclusive and diverse, hopefully, the so-called alternative or complementary medicines will be increasingly accepted by the policy-makers and the public.

In Chapter 4, we will look at another facet of Indian culture that used to be a prominent part of pop culture but now is limited to the counter-culture, marginalized in the American media. There was a time when Ravi Shankar, for instance, was a popular name in America. Chapter 4 surveys the influence of Indian classical music on America and describes its current status.

Notes

1 See https://sites.sph.harvard.edu/wmy/celebrities/deepak-chopra/ (accessed May 12, 2019).
2 See www.cnn.com/profiles/sanjay-gupta-profile (accessed May 12, 2019).
3 See www.newyorker.com/contributors/atul-gawande (accessed May 12, 2019).
4 See https://sources.npr.org/vivek-murthy/ (accessed May 12, 2019).
5 A 1979 study published in the *American Journal of Public Health* demonstrated no difference in performance of International Medical Graduates (IMGs) and US Medical Graduates (USMGs) (Saywell et al., 1979). However, IMGs still had to campaign for years to achieve equity and equality in various areas of medical practice.
6 Due to the sustained efforts of Indian doctors, one important change worth mentioning is the removal of the clause that used to prohibit screening patients for prostate cancer after the age of 70. After urologists from AAPI approached some US Senators and Black Caucus, a new law was passed in 2012, that now allows doctors to decide on these tests, giving better benefits to senior citizens.
7 They are Gauri Junnarkar Chaudhuri, Sapna Punjabi-Gupta, Meenakshi Gupta, Amba Prabhakar, and Dhanada Kulkarni.
8 See https://santhigramusa.com/texas/ (accessed May 13, 2019).
9 See http://astangaayurvedcenter.com/?post_type=template&p=10858 (accessed May 13, 2019).
10 See www.indianspices.com/ (accessed May 13, 2019).
11 See http://indianspices.com/sites/default/files/cou172018123_new.pdf (accessed May 13, 2019).
12 See www.dallasobserver.com/restaurants/the-story-of-cosmic-cafe-a-vegetarian-dallas-institution-9962364 (accessed May 13, 2019).
13 See https://restaurant.org/Articles/News/North-African-cuisine-among-top-global-flavors (accessed May 13, 2019).
14 See www.medicalnewstoday.com/articles/282929.php (accessed May 11, 2019).
15 See https://open.lib.umn.edu/socialproblems/chapter/13-4-problems-of-health-care-in-the-united-states/ (accessed May 11, 2019).

4   Indian classical and Hindu music in America

Like Indian doctors or Ayurveda, Indian classical music (ICM) and Indian musicians in America, are also not often mentioned in academic books about the Indian diaspora except for a passing reference to Zubin Mehta[1] or Ravi Shankar.[2] One of the earliest short academic introductions to ICM by Priya Chatterji can be seen in the 1958 issue of an Italian journal *East and West*. As this book's focus is Indians and Indian culture in America, this chapter surveys the history of ICM in North America and leaves out many European interactions with ICM that can be found in excellent surveys such as by Alison Arnold (2015) and Peter Lavezzoli (2007). In this chapter, one will find more information about ICM in America from the 1950s to the 1970s and fewer details about developments after the 1970s because the golden period of ICM in America was indeed those couple of decades with the charismatic figures such as Ravi Shankar and Ali Akbar Khan. Unfortunately, ICM never continued to achieve that mainstream appeal afterward, as we will see in this chapter. Before we delve into the history of ICM in America, let us take a look at what ICM is.

A very short introduction to Indian classical music (ICM)

Like many elements of Indian heritage, my first encounter with ICM happened not in India, but the United States. As is true of almost all Indian communities across North America, New Jersey has its group of ICM schools. One such school is the Academy of Indian Music in Edison, where I learned about ICM from one of the teachers Manoj Govindraj.[3] Although ICM has a millennia-old history with references in the oldest Hindu texts, such as the *Vedas* and the *Natyashastra*, it was categorized into the Hindustani (North Indian) and Carnatic (South Indian) systems a few centuries ago. Both systems produce intricate melodies based on *raga* and *tala*. A *raga* is a pattern of notes with different intervals and pitches, and a *tala* refers to the musical meter or rhythm. Both *raga* and *tala* have been combined by vocalists and instrumentalists to create hundreds of melodies for many centuries, many of which are also categorized according to the season of the year or the time of the day or mood of the artist performing. For instance, *ragas* such as Bhairav and Yaman are sung in the morning, and evening, respectively.

Pioneer Indian classical musicians in America

Gerry Farrell's 1997 monograph on this subject has some interesting insights. In the fifth chapter, he mentions that as early as 1910, Sufi *Veena* player Hazrat Inayat Khan (1882–1927) brought ICM to the USA with his team, "The Royal Musicians of Hindustan." Professor P. M.C. Rybner, the chair of the Music Department at Columbia University in New York City, hosted Khan's performance and admired the "scientific nature" of ICM. Although Khan, and later his other family members, traveled widely in America and the European countries and interacted with various Western musicians, he eventually discouraged the spread of Indian music outside the "strict boundaries of audiences' musical taste and education" (Arnold 2015). However, his path-breaking contributions to bring ICM to the West paved the way for later similar efforts. Farrell also describes the similar "missions" by Rabindranath Tagore (1861–1941) and Uday Shankar (1900–1977), the precursor and older brother of legendary sitarist Ravi Shankar (1920–2012). Both Rabindranath Tagore and Uday Shankar introduced Western influences in their future creations upon their return to India (Abrahams 1986). All these earliest ICM pioneers intertwined their music with their mission to bring Indian culture and also spirituality to the West. A great example of such observation is the statement by Yehudi Menuhin in his Introduction to Ravi Shankar's autobiography. Menuhin states, "Indian music is an exalted expression of union with the infinite which few modern composers in the West have achieved" (Farrell 1997, 170). In 1924, Anna Pavlova, the famous Russian dancer, noticed Uday Shankar's dance in an Indian performance organized by his father in London. That quickly led to their collaboration and even a tour to the United States in 1929. One of the earliest milestones of ICM's arrival in North America is noted by Farrell (ibid., 166) when, in 1939, Dorothy and Leonard Elmhirst opened an account with American Express in the name of the "Uday Shankar India Culture Trust."

In 1955, the famous violinist Yehudi Menuhin invited Ravi Shankar to perform in New York's Museum of Modern Art (MoMA) at the festival "The Living Arts of India." Instead of Ravi Shankar accepting this invitation, he recommended the equally accomplished sarod maestro Ali Akbar Khan and the accompanists Chaturlal on tabla and Shirish Gor on tamboura. Satyajit Ray's film *Pather Panchali*, that featured Ravi Shankar's music, was also shown as a part of the festival for several weeks (Lavezzoli 2007, 58). After the festival, Ali Akbar Khan and Chaturlal teamed up with Shanta Rao, a Bharatanatyam dancer, to also appear in one of the episodes of a TV series *Omnibus*,[4] funded by the Ford Foundation that had sponsored their trip from India.

The collaboration among these artists, i.e., Yehudi Menuhin, Ravi Shankar, and Ali Akbar Khan, that started in the 1950s continued for the next several years. In 1955, the first-ever album of ICM, *Music of India: Morning and Evening Ragas* was released, with an introduction by Yehudi Menuhin (Lavezzoli 2007, 1), featuring the Indian sarod maestro Ali Akbar Khan, and it was issued on Angel Records, a record label founded by EMI in 1953. Among its tracks, Raga Sindhu Bhairavi presented the morning *raga*, and Raga Pilu was selected to play an evening *raga*. In 1995, the album was reissued as *Ali Akbar Khan: Then and Now* and was nominated for a Grammy Award. Lavezzoli opens his 2007 book about ICM in the West with a fantastic introduction to this album. He appropriately calls this album that begins with the morning *raga* Sindhu Bhairavi the "dawn" of ICM in the West. He also notes that this album was recorded at MoMA (the Museum of Modern Art) on April 18 just a day before the first concert by Khan and his team. On April 18, after the recording, both Menuhin and Khan jointly celebrated their birthdays falling before and after April 18 respectively. Like the album, the concert was widely admired by the media, such as *The New York Times* and *The New Yorker*. Ali Akbar Khan and his team gave a couple more shows, including one in Washington, DC, to celebrate India's 50th Independence Day, and returned very satisfied to India only to return to the United States soon after with Ravi Shankar. Ali Akbar Khan was honored with multiple awards in the United States, such as by Padma Vibhushan in 1989 in India, a MacArthur Fellowship in 1991, and a National Heritage Fellowship by the National Endowment for the Arts in 1997.

Lavezzoli notes another milestone in the ICM journey to be the Grammy-winning album *West Meets East* by Ravi Shankar and Yehudi Menuhin. Lavezzoli (ibid., 61) also recollects Ravi Shankar's very first album *Three Ragas* from 1956 that included a North Indian *raga* Jog and a Carnatic *raga* Simhendra Madhyamam, a pioneering attempt to include both styles, according to Lavezzoli. EMI released the album in London. Ravi Shankar released his next album *Sounds of India* with Columbia in 1957 with *raga* Bihag, Bhimpalasi, and Sindhu Bhairavi. Also, on his first trip to the US, Ravi Shankar met Richard Bock, the founder of World Pacific Records, at his concert at the Self Realization Fellowship Center in Los Angeles. Bock produced several albums for Ravi Shankar in the 1950s and the 1960s. This collaboration was followed by Ravi Shankar's next collaboration with the Beatles. Meanwhile, in 1957, Dr. Rosette Renshaw introduced Ravi Shankar to the Canadian CBC Television network and soon launched the ICM program at McGill University where he invited Ali Akbar Khan to perform several times.

Wade (1978, 30) describes the album with the title *Music of India II* that also featured Ravi Shankar with three *ragas*. Shankar told a reporter in 1967 that ICM provided a new system of music and spirituality to the Western youth and George Harrison later said the same thing to another reporter. At that time, Shankar felt that his educational mission was now complete, and he could play the music as he pleased instead of worrying about educating his audience (ibid., 35–37).

As a young boy aged 10, Ravi Shankar already accompanied his older brother Uday Shankar and his band in 1932 in their first performance in New York. George Harrison, the lead guitarist of the Beatles, is credited as being the first Western musician to incorporate an Indian instrument, sitar as a substitute guitar, in one of his tracks, "Norwegian Wood," on the Beatles' *Rubber Soul* album (Farrell 1997, 171), most likely after Harrison met Ravi Shankar and began taking sitar lessons from him in 1966 (ibid., 183). Some of the most famous Beatles songs, "Blue Jay Way" and "The Inner Light," were heavily influenced by Indian music and culture. Farrell cites this quote by Harrison (ibid., 188):

> With pop music, the more you listen to it, the more you get to know it, the more you see through it and the less satisfaction it gives you, whereas with Indian music and Ravi Shankar as a person, it's exactly the opposite because the more you're able to understand the music, the more you see there is to appreciate. The more you get back out of it. You can have just one record of Indian music and play it for the rest of your life and you probably still never see all the subtleties in it.

As jazz was already open to Indian, Islamic, and African music, Ravi Shankar started working with jazz musicians in 1961 in California, even before Indian music became fashionable in pop music. The result of this collaboration with flutist Bud Shank, Paul Horn, and others was the album *Improvisations*. The album contained traditional Indian classical *ragas* and many other pieces for jazz and Indian music groups. Other prominent jazz musicians who incorporated Indian music and cultural elements included John Coltrane, Harihar Rao, Don Ellis, Ralph Towner, the late Colin Walcott of the group Oregon, and saxophonist Charlie Mariano, with each developing ways to incorporate the elements of ICM. 1961 also saw glowing journalistic accounts, including one in *The New Yorker*, of Ravi Shankar's concert in New York (Wade 1978, 31).

By the end of the 1960s, Ravi Shankar was performing at huge concerts such as the Monterey Pop Festival in California with other rock stars but his zenith, "The Great Sitar Explosion," was the five months between May and September 1966 (Farrell 1997, 177). Shankar was also one of the earliest Indian musicians to teach ICM to the audience in America. He not only corrected their misconceptions but also expected appropriate behavior and participation from them, for instance, by prohibiting alcohol consumption in his concerts. He also started the tradition of maintaining a visually appealing stage with decent furniture and sufficient light. Most ICM artists have continued to perform on a similar dais ever since (Slawek 1993, 165). In 1967, he opened a school for Indian music called *Kinnara*, but that closed after a few years (Arnold 2015). When George Harrison collaborated with Ravi Shankar, it opened new vistas for ICM. Harrison continued to experiment with Indian music until 1970, even after the Beatles disbanded (Farrell 1997, 176–178).

Ravi Shankar performed with Alla Rakha (a famous tabla player) at the Monterey Pop Festival in 1967 and the Woodstock Festival in 1969, further increasing their popularity. In 1969, they performed live at the San Francisco Civic Auditorium (now known as the Bill Graham Civic Auditorium). The performance there was recorded and was released as an album *Ravi Shankar in San Francisco* with a couple of *ragas* by Shankar and a solo by Allah Rakha. Lavezzoli counts this album as one of the best tabla performances ever. Just before this recording, Rakha released a trend-setting album with a jazz musician Buddy Rich, entitled *Rich a la Rakha* in 1968, the music on it was composed by Ravi Shankar. This album paved the way for many similar future collaborative efforts between Indian and Western musicians, including by Rakha's equally legendary son, Zakir Hussain, who transcended many more boundaries in his illustrious career also as a tablaist. Rakha opened his music school in Mumbai in 1985 and eventually stopped his trips abroad. Before his international travels, Alla Rakha also composed music for Hindi films under his family name, A. R. Qureshi. Some of his movies included *Bewafa* (1947), *Laila* (1954), *Khandaan* (1955), and *Alam Ara* (1956). However, it was his exclusive collaboration with Shankar from 1962 to 1985 that will remain most memorable in the history of ICM (Lavezzoli 2007, 103).

Zakir Hussain started learning and performing as the young prodigious son of his legendary father, All Rakha. In 1970, Ravi Shankar was scheduled to play for the third time at the prestigious rock avenue Fillmore East, with Alla Rakha as his regular companion. When suddenly Rakha fell ill, Shankar invited his son Hussain. This New York event launched Hussain in America. He soon found himself as an ethnomusicology faculty at the University of Washington in Seattle, where he learned other world music genres in addition to teaching ICM. Within two years, Khan invited Hussain to join his college AACM in California. In 1972, Hussain released an album, *Rolling Thunder*, with Mickey Hart, a friend of Alla Rakha.

Unlike on pop music, ICM had a more in-depth and long-lasting impact on jazz, partly as a coincidence of its arrival in the 1950s and the 1960s when jazz musicians were experimenting with newer and different kinds of music at the structural level. For instance, since the late 1960s, John McLaughlin had been interested in both Indian music and Indian culture. In 1970, he became a follower of a Hindu guru living in the USA, Sri Chinmoy, who was also interested in presenting Indian music to a Western audience. McLaughlin learned the Indian musical instrument veena and composed several albums inspired by his guru's teachings. In his records, *My Goal's Beyond* (1971) and *Love Devotion Surrender* (1973), McLaughlin played acoustic guitar with tanpura and tabla as supporting instruments. In 1971, he launched the *Mahavishnu Orchestra*, based on his new name given by his guru Chinmoy. This group had several incarnations and released several albums with influences from Indian music. In 1970, McLaughlin briefly met Zakir Hussain in New York and was impressed by his tabla performance. In 1972, while on tour with the *Mahavishnu Orchestra*, McLaughlin met Hussain at Ali Akbar Khan's house in California that paved the way for several collaborations between them. In 1975, John McLaughlin launched a new group *Shakti* with Zakir Hussain, violinist L. Shankar, and percussionist T. H. Vinayakram. L. Shankar, Vinayakram and Hussain collaborated on many more albums, including *Who's to Know* (1980), *Song for Everyone* (1985), *Nobody Told Me* (1989), and *Eternal Light* (2000). Many other experiments took place in which Indian music was incorporated into jazz, such as the works by Coltrane, Indo Jazz Fusions, the Hindustani Jazz Sextet, and others. In 1976, the album, *Diga Rhythm Band*, was released by Hussain and Mickey Hart that featured several of Hussain's students from AACM. Hussain married one of the earliest Western Kathak dancers Antonia Minnecola, who performed with him several times and also continues to manage Hussain's busy career. In 1986, Hussain released *Making Music* with Hariprasad Chaurasia on flute and John McLaughlin on acoustic guitar. In 1991, he established his recording company *Moment! Records* in California. Some of the notable albums released by this company include Ravi Shankar's *Concert for Peace* (1995) and Amjad Ali Khan's *Homage to Mother Teresa* (1999).

In 1994, he released *Masters of Percussions* featuring several great international percussionists. In 1999, Zakir Hussain and Bill Laswell co-founded a musical group called *Tabla Beat Science*. According to Dixit (2002):

> Such collaborative efforts of Zakir Hussain with musicians from various other genres of music, such as Western classical, African, Jazz, Pop, Rock, and Folk brought him and Indian Classical Music, particularly the percussion part of it, unprecedented visibility in North America. His association with L. Shankar, T. H. Vinayakram, and John McLaughlin made a large number of music enthusiasts from the West aware of some aspects of Indian Classical Music.

He also acted in or composed music for several Indian and American films, such as *Apocalypse Now* (1979), *In Custody* (1994), *Saaz* (1997), *The Mystic Masseur* (2001), *Mr. and Mrs. Iyer* (2002), and *Parzania* (2005). Hussain has also been a visiting scholar at universities, such as Stanford and Princeton. Menuhin, Shankar, Khan, Rakha, and Harrison collaborated in various ways on international programs, such as the Concert for Bangladesh (1971), to raise funds for UNESCO's humanitarian programs in Bangladesh, and at United Nations' Human Rights Day. The album *The Concert for Bangladesh* won a Grammy Award for Album of the Year and remained one of the highest-selling recordings featuring ICM (Lavezzoli 2007, 9).

Ravi Shankar also wrote art music (concertos) for sitar and orchestra that were included in the programs of Western ensembles. His former student, Professor Stephen Slawek, fondly recalled the second such concerto called *Raga Mala* in 1979 with the New York Philharmonic Orchestra, organized at the request of the leading conductor Zubin Mehta.[5] The concerto contained more than two dozen *ragas* of ICM in four successive movements. Shankar's *Concerto No. 1* remains popular in the West, but *Raga Mala* has rarely been performed again although Angel Records released its recording in 1982 (Slawek 1993, 176).

He also composed music for several documentaries and feature films in Bengali, Hindi, and English, such as *Neecha Nagar* (1946), *Dharti Ke Lal* (1946), *Apu Trilogy* (1955–1959), *Kabuliwala* (1957), *Anuradha* (1960), Godaan (1963), *Charly* (1968), *Meera* (1979), *Gandhi* (1982), and *Genesis* (1986). His other experimentations included *The Ravi Shankar Project, Passages* with the minimalist composer Philip Glass, and *Svar Milan* with Russian artists (ibid., 163). Another famous sitar player, Nikhil Banerjee also joined in some of the concerts. In 2000, Ravi Shankar received his third Grammy for *Full Circle*, a live recording from New York's Carnegie Hall, with his daughter Anoushka Shankar.

The founders of the American Society for Eastern Arts (ASEA), based in Oakland, California, Samuel and Louise Scripps invited Ali Akbar Khan to teach ICM in 1965. As Khan's courses became exceedingly popular, in 1967, Khan opened the Ali Akbar College of Music (AACM) at Berkeley (and later moved to more peaceful Marin County) in California (Khan 2018). This school was the US branch of his Calcutta-based College of Music. The initial support for the college came from the Buddhist scholar Allan Watts and his wealthy friends. In 1968, Khan began teaching vocal and sarod with a few more musicians from India for the next several decades. Several renowned musicians also taught at this college that is now managed by Swapan Chaudhuri and continues to attract a large number of American students. Besides teaching and performing, Ali Akbar Khan also composed music for several documentaries and Bengali, Hindi, and English films such as *Aandhiyan* (1954), *Devi* (1960), and *The Householder* (1963).

American pianist Keith Jarrett also incorporated influences from ICM in his music (Blume 2003). According to Lakshmi Subramaniam (2008), in North America, UCLA pioneered the Carnatic music instruction in 1958, followed by Wesleyan University that started offering similar courses in 1961. Nazir Jairazbhoy was UCLA's first ICM faculty and the founding chair of the Department of Ethnomusicology and Systematic Musicology. His student Peter Manuel continues teaching ICM at the City University of New York.

In 1971, Trichy Sankaran and Jon Higgins co-founded a similar program at York University in Canada. The Cleveland festival transplanted Thyagaraja Utsavam, an Indian classical music festival of South India, to the United States in the 1970s with great success. Such early initiatives were primarily due to the general interest of the American public in Hindu culture and music. The most notable Carnatic performance was in 1966 by M. S. Subbulakshmi at the UN General Assembly.[6] Her performance was steeped in Hindu devotional lyrics penned by her guru Chandrashekharendra Saraswati of Kanchipuram. Although her performance was appreciated by the UN Secretary-General and was reported in *The New York Times*, only in 1977 did she return to the USA to perform at the Carnegie Hall in New York.[7]

Indian immigrants' impetus for ICM teaching and performances

Indian immigrants started initiatives such as the Carnatic Music Association of North America CMANA[8] in 1976, "to serve as a cultural-bridge that promotes and propagates the learning, understanding, performing, and appreciation of the Carnatic style of ICM and related fine arts in North America." CMANA patrons include eminent musicians and scholars such as T. N. Bala, Robert Browning of the World Music Institute (WMI), Guruvayoor Durai, Harold Powers of Princeton University, David Reck of Amherst University, Ramnad Raghavan, and T. Viswanathan (both from Chennai and Wesleyan University). Other prominent ICM organizations include the Indian Classical Music Circle in Dallas (established in 1983), the Indian Music Society in Houston (established in 1992), Kalalaya in California (established in 1992), Bhairavi in Cleveland, Ohio (established in 2001), and Ragamala in Seattle (established in 1981).

This combination of American and Indian immigrants' interest in ICM produced some innovative trends. For instance, T. Viswanathan succeeded in developing an alternative classical tradition that combined his ancestral musical tradition experimentally with other forms of music available in America. Ranga Ramanuja Ayyangar designed a course at Jefferson College, Michigan, in 1972 that led to three public recitals by the "TJC Carnatic Ensemble," an American group with five veenas, clarinet, cello, flute, vocal music, and Konakkol accompaniment for rhythm. Unlike the Indian immigrants who were mostly interested in ICM for social or art or entertainment reasons, Americans were more interested in Hindu/Indian spirituality intertwined with Indian music. In the 1970s, Ayyangar developed the Dhanam style as the classical South Indian music in the United States as an alternative to the Indian-based Madras Music Academy style, of which he remained a critic (ibid.).

In 1961, the program in Carnatic Music was started by the ethnomusicologist Robert Brown at Wesleyan University in Connecticut after he received his PhD from UCLA and later traveled to Madras (now Chennai). The program began with the hiring of the great mridangam (a traditional percussion instrument) artist T. Ranganathan, who was later joined by his siblings and other South Indian artists (Slawek 1993, 166). Jon B. Higgins was one of the earliest American students and scholars of this program[9] and was first noted in his concert of at Carnegie Hall in May 1964 and 1965 at the Thyagaraja Festival. On a Fulbright Fellowship, he studied in India under T. Viswanathan, one of India's foremost musicians ,who later joined Higgins at Wesleyan University as an artist-in-residence. Higgins went on to teach at the University of Minnesota and York University before returning to his Alma Mater, Wesleyan University, to join as faculty. Wesleyan is thus the oldest American university teaching ICM with several South and North Indian artists as visiting artists and scholars over the years.[10] In 1974, two leading South Indian musicians completed their doctorates at Wesleyan, and they were L. Shankar and Ramanathan.

Similarly, at the University of Pennsylvania, Harold Powers started teaching ICM in 1961 after receiving his PhD in 1959 from Princeton University in the South Indian Raga System. Dr. Lalmani Mishra and Jnan Prakash Ghosh, in 1969, were among the visiting artists and scholars from India.

At the Massachusetts Institute of Technology (MIT), MITHAS was founded in 1993 by the senior music lecturer George Ruckert, MIT alumni Moez Rawji, and Donald Chand to bring quality Indian classical music to the Boston area. MITHAS has performed more than 150 concerts and lectures of Carnatic and Hindustani music and dance as of 2019. Its advisory board has included Ali Akbar Khan, Ravi Shankar, Zubin Mehta, Bonnie Wade, Zakir Hussain, Swapan Chaudhuri, and others. The MITHAS series of concerts opened with vocalist Rashid Khan in February 1993, and they have hosted many great artists, as well as many less well-known and western artists. Prominent Hindustani artists include Ali Akbar Khan, Pandit Jasraj, Zakir Hussain, Rajan and Sajan Mishra, Hari Prasad Chaurasia, Ajoy Chakrabarty and his daughter Kaushiki, Kartik Seshadri, Uday Bhawalkar, Gundecha Brothers, Shahid Parvez, Kushal Das, Prabha Atre, Manilal Nag, Mita Nag, Ramesh Mishra, Nayan Ghosh, Tejendra Majumdar, Swapan Chaudhuri, and numerous others. Carnatic artists hosted by MITHAS include T.M. Krishna, Balamuralikrishna, Bombay Jayashri, Malladi Brothers, T. V. Sankaranarayanan, Unnikrishnan, Sanjay Subrahmanyan, Mandolin Srinivas, and many others. George Ruckert also emphasized the importance of Western scholars (such as Allyn Miner, a sitarist who teaches at the University of Pennsylvania) and others who have written about Indian music from a Western perspective. For instance, the Indian Musicological Society was for many years centered in Amsterdam and attracted many American contributors; the Ali Akbar College of Music in Basel, Switzerland, is headed by an American sarodist, Ken Zuckerman; Chhandika and Chhandam, Kathak dance schools in the USA, are Indo-American; Joanna de Souza teaches Kathak in Toronto, etc. According to Ruckert, "ICM is now an international art form, and now national boundaries have even a slightly biased claim on ownership and development. Just like Yo-Yo Ma, Seiji Ozawa, and even Yoga, national origins do not circumscribe the arts" (2004, 17).

Ever since the California Institute of the Arts was established with the support of the Walt Disney Foundation, the North Indian Music Graduate Program has been an integral program there, with Ravi Shankar being the inaugural faculty and Swapan Chaudhuri being the department chairperson for the World Music Department in 2018. Also, UCLA, UC Berkeley (by Bonnie Wade in 1975), the University of Washington (by Robert Garfias in the early 1960s), Amherst College and the University of Texas at Austin started their academic programs on ICM, and most of them have continued till the present time. Although Princeton University, UC Berkeley, the University of Illinois at Urbana Champagne, and San Diego State University did not replace their Indianists, other universities such as Stanford University, Harvard University, the University of Minnesota, the University of Cincinnati, the University of

Denver, and the University of North Texas have hired ethnomusicologists who are all experts in some aspects of ICM.

Established in 1975 in Canada, the Raga-Mala Music Society of Calgary promotes ICM and dance. It has presented more than two hundred performances of music and dance of artists from both Hindustani and Carnatic traditions. Several similar organizations such as the Music Circle (California, established in 1973), the World Music Institute (New York, established in 1985), Basant Bahar (California, established in 1982), the Indian Music Society (Minnesota, established in 1980), Kalakendra (Oregon, established in 1987), the Indian Classical Music Circle (Texas, established in 1983), the Cleveland Thyagaraja Festival (Ohio, established in 1978), Sangeetha (Missouri, established in 1984), and the Indian Music Society (Texas, established in 1992), and Sruti (Pennsylvania, established in 1986) have promoted ICM in their respective local cities and suburbs.

In the early 1980s, films such as *Gandhi* and *A Passage to India* and TV series such as *The Jewel in the Crown* helped arouse American interest in India. The Indian government sought to build on this by organizing the yearlong Festival of India in 1985.[11] As part of this festival, the Indian Council for Cultural Relations (ICCR), ITC's Sangeet Research Academy (SRA), and the University of Pittsburgh collaborated to organize over 90 concerts and over 25 workshops by more than 20 top musicians from both Hindustani and Carnatic styles. As a legacy of this effort, ICCR signed a contract with the University of Pittsburgh to establish the "University Circuit for Indian Classical Music" and presented about 20 concerts by various Indian musicians at about 75 universities and colleges in the next five years. The "circuit" was then expanded into the Center for the Performing Arts of India (CPAI). According to its founder Dixit (2002), about 70–120 concerts of Hindustani music were presented annually to audiences throughout the USA, raising over $1.7 million from the public without any funding support from the University of Pittsburgh. Over the years, it organized over 70 concert tours with 1,600 concerts and 300 workshops. Since Carnatic music was already promoted by other organizations, it focused on Hindustani music for most of its programs. According to Dixit (ibid.), the national sponsors prepare the documentation for Indian artists' visas, travel arrangements, health insurance, and US income tax returns. National organizations such as CPAI depend on several local organizations that host the visiting artists from India and are supported by local donations from Indian Americans and funding from local government agencies. From March to November, since concerts are rare in India then due to the monsoon season, a large number of musicians travel to North America for shows during this period. Most programs continue to be attended mainly by Indian Americans and not many other ethnicities, except at university campuses.

Dixit also notes the contributions of online newsgroups such as rec. music.indian.classical and several other websites on different musicians. These additional resources are increasingly helpful as many artists find it difficult to explain their classical music to an interested audience in a workshop setting. Dixit also notes that Carnatic music is better supported by organizations and temples representing Indians from southern states than Hindustani music.

In Canada, Dr. Vinay Bhide has been teaching ICM at Carleton University since 2002. Trichy Sankaran is the founding director of ICM Studies at York University. Shawn Mativetsky is an ICM percussionist at McGill University. According to Dr. Bhide, people in France and French-speaking people in Canada are more interested in ICM than English-speaking people.

Due to the pioneering efforts by great artists such as the Hindustani instrumentalists Ali Akbar Khan and Amjad Ali Khan (sarod), Bismillah Khan (shehnai), Nikhil Banerjee and Imrat Khan (sitar), Ram Narayan (sarangi), Zakir Hussain (tabla), and the Carnatic artists T. Viswanathan (flute), T. Ranganathan (mridangam), and M. S. Subbulakshmi (voice), ICM continues to be found in its various elements such as the sounds of tabla and sitar that are increasingly heard in jazz, pop, and rock music, though for most Western audiences, ICM performers remain exotic and rare (Arnold 2015). According to Neuman (1984, 14), the characteristics of ICM that have helped its acceptance in the Western context include ICM's high cultural status in India, its connection with Indian spirituality, its flexibility to adapt to different kinds of audience, and its ease of transportation due to the small size of its group performers. Indophiles and the Indian diaspora in the West are also contributing to maintain ICM as a viable tradition in the West. Wade (1978, 33) further elaborates the specific innovations that Ravi Shankar used that helped him succeed enormously in the West. First, he halved the duration of his performances and then he divided them into two parts. The first half typically is shorter than the second longer part that could be enjoyed by the late-comers also. Shankar continued his longer performances for more seriously interested audiences. His earlier trips with his older brother had already prepared him to be the first primary ICM ambassador to the West. Also, Shankar had two significant Western musician colleagues, who both contributed to his success in different ways. While Yehudi Menuhin helped Shankar reach the Western classical music audience, George Harrison helped him reach the Western popular music audience.

Music of Bhajan and Kirtan

Let us now turn to another category of musical performances that is popularly known as *Bhajan* and *Kirtan* (Beck 2010; 2013). In addition to hundreds of Hindu, Jain, and Sikh temples in North America built and managed by Indian immigrants, several yoga centers now incorporate this kind of music in their practices. In her 2016 MA thesis, Patrick Bowe Kyle presents a moving account of her transformation with her practice of Yoga and Kirtan with different teachers (Kyle 2016). Every year during the last weekend in March, the local Hare Krishna community in small-town Spanish Fork, Utah, hosts what is arguably the most significant Hindu festival in the United States. In recent years the Utah Festival of Colors has drawn crowds of as large as 65,000 people. The Utah Festival of Colors, held at the Sri Radha Krishna temple, is a celebration of the Indian festival of Holi. The tradition of observing Holi in Utah was established in the early 1980s by the temple president Caru Das with a group he remembers as comprising "maybe five Indians, three BYU students, and six [Krishna] devotees" (Brown, 2012; 2014).

Some of the global Indic guru movements have also been incorporating Bhajan and Kirtan extensively. We have already noted the interactions of the Beatles and George Harrison with Maharishi Mahesh Yogi and ISKCON. Coincidentally, as I was writing this chapter, Shantamrita Chaitanya, the central zone coordinator for the "hugging saint" Amma's Mata Amritanandamayi Mission Trust in North America, invited me to visit their newly inaugurated center in Denton, near my university. As I visited this center in the "horse country" of Northern Texas,[12] I also started visiting their different websites and read the monograph by Amanda Lucia (2014). As of 2019, there are similar centers in California, Illinois, Michigan, Iowa, Massachusetts, New Mexico, Washington, DC, and Arkansas. Also, there are centers in other North and South American countries such as Canada, Chile, Argentina, Brazil, Venezuela, and Mexico. Devotional music remains an integral part of all of their activities.

Amma sings in several Indian and international languages whenever she conducts her darshan and embracing ceremonies with thousands of her disciples across the world (Raj 2004). The first page of their website, www.Amritapuri.org shows a picture of Amma singing, with the quote stating, "Pure music is as big as space. It is the secret of allowing the pure sound of the universe to flow through you." All her coordinators and regional leaders also coordinate the Bhajan and Kirtan events in their respective regions. A Google search for "Amma bhajans" showed more than 366,000 hits with long playlists of her more than 1,000 bhajans in 35 world languages on her own websites such as www.sing.withamma.com (Fibiger 2017) as well as other popular sites such as YouTube, SoundCloud, Spotify, Amazon Music, Facebook, Google Play, and iTunes. On another official Amma website, her teachings encourage her disciples to sing bhajans:

> To gain concentration in this age of materialism, bhajan is easier than meditation. By loud singing, other distracting sounds will be overcome, and concentration will be achieved. Bhajan, concentration, and meditation, this is the progression. Constant remembrance of God is meditation. Bhajans, sung with one-pointedness will benefit the singer, the listener, and also Mother Nature. Such songs will awaken the listeners' minds in due course.[13]

Some of the centers occasionally conduct workshops, classes, and retreats to teach music to their devotees.

I attended the *Satsang*, the spiritual gathering, on February 26, 2019, at their Denton center in Texas. In a usual call and response group singing pattern, Shantamrita Chaitanya led the group in a bhajan session for about an hour in which he played the harmonium, and one of the female devotees played a small hand-held drum. The *Satsang* began with the chanting of Sanskrit verses dedicated to their guru, i.e., Amma. The first bhajan they sang was in Malayalam, the second in Telugu, the third in Hindi, and finally a Kannada bhajan. All of the bhajans were published in beautiful little booklets in which lyrics were transliterated in English with their translations. For each bhajan, I was shown the relevant pages to follow, while the rest of the group referred to the electronic versions of these booklets on their smartphones or tablets. After the session, I was told that they always sing bhajans in different languages in almost all of their *satsangs*. Another Hindu global movement that shows similar musical practices is the International Sathya Sai Baba Organization, on whose website thousands of bhajans in English, Hebrew, Hindi, Telugu, Tamil, Spanish, and Japanese are available.

Conclusion

In the so-called globalized world of the twenty-first century, Indian (and other non-Western) musical traditions continue to be categorized as "ethnomusicology" while only Western music is classified as "normal" music in most American colleges or schools of music. However, beyond the boundaries of academia, Indian music is greatly flourishing, especially in the last century when the stalwarts such as Ravi Shankar and others made America reverberate with their musical geniuses. In the twenty-first century, Indian music continues to thrive not only in the Indian immigrant circles but also continues to echo in spiritual gatherings inspired by Hindu traditions. As some of the other disciplines, such as religious studies, have become more diversified and inclusive, musicology will also continue to broaden for its future students.

Having seen the arrival and impact of Indian doctors, Ayurveda, and Indian classical music, we now turn to the history of Jain Americans in Chapter 5. Jainism, a small minority in India, remains a small minority within Indian Americans in North America with an estimated only 150,000 Jains in America.[14]

Notes

1 See www.britannica.com/biography/Zubin-Mehta (accessed May 12, 2019).
2 See www.britannica.com/biography/Ravi-Shankar (accessed May 12, 2019).
3 See http://aimarts.org/aimarts_music_faculty.html (accessed May 12, 2019).
4 See www.imdb.com/title/tt0044284/ (accessed May 13, 2019).
5 Zubin Mehta is one of the most accomplished Indian American artists of Western music. See, Dadabhoy, Bakhtiar. *Zubin Mehta: A Musical Journey* (Gurgaon, India: Penguin Viking, 2016).

6 See www.thebetterindia.com/68450/m-s-subbulakshmi-concert-united-nations/ (accessed January 19, 2018).

7 See www.nytimes.com/1977/10/21/archives/new-jersey-weekly-music-indias-best-woman-singer.html (accessed May 13, 2019).

8 See www.cmana.org/Introduction-p-1-about (accessed January 19, 2018).

9 See www.nytimes.com/1984/12/09/obituaries/jon-b-higgins-expert-in-south-indian-music.html (accessed May 13, 2019).

10 See www.thehindu.com/features/friday-review/music/Carnatic-music-in-America-then-and-now/article15605571.ece (accessed January 19, 2018).

11 See www.nytimes.com/1985/05/05/us/festival-in-capital-a-taste-of-india.html (accessed January 28, 2018).

12 See https://amma.org/groups/north-america/macenter-dallas/about (accessed February 25, 2019).

13 See https://amma.org/teachings/why-singing-spiritual-practice (accessed February 25, 2019).

14 http://www.jainology.org/congratulations-to-vinodbhai/ (accessed May 13, 2019)

5 Jains in North America

Introduction

Although the financial media occasionally mention the names of Ajit Jain[1] and Anshu Jain,[2] as a couple of high-ranking executives working in major American corporations, Jainism remains one of the least known and least practiced phenomena in the Americas. Jainism is one of the oldest Indic religious traditions, along with Hinduism and Buddhism, with a history of at least 2,600 years. The word Jain, often the last name for its practitioners, is derived from the word Jina that means the one who has conquered their beings, including their bodies, passions, and desires. All Jains are followers of such conquerors, Jinas. Although the total number of Jains are recorded to be less than 10 million in the world, their social, political, and economic influence in India has been noted for millennia. Although Ashoka, the best-known ancient Indian emperor, embraced Buddhism, both his grandfather and his grandson embraced Jainism in their later age, at least according to the Jain sources. Even the Islamic emperors, such as Akbar and his son Jehangir, hosted Jain monks and at least partially accepted one of the most widely known Jain principles of nonviolence (*ahimsa*) that is practiced in the form of vegetarianism. In addition to nonviolence, the other four Jain principles are truth (*satya*), not to steal (*asteya*), not to accumulate (*aparigraha*), and celibacy (*brahmacharaya*). These five vows are practiced to the ultimate level by the Jain monks and nuns. However, for lay Jains, the rules are relaxed and are practiced in their minor form.

Because of the great emphasis on nonviolence in Jainism, traveling was discouraged historically, especially for the ascetics. For the past 2,600 years, Jain monks and nuns have never used any vehicle for their travel and even today they only walk to travel from one town or village to the other and to collect their food in the form of alms. Except for the rainy season, they keep moving in different regions for the rest of the eight months to prevent any attachment to a specific place or its people and to keep spreading the message of nonviolence among the masses. However, unlike Hinduism and Buddhism that spread across Asia, Jainism had a limited extent, mostly in Northern, Southern, and Western parts of India. As the Indian diaspora became a global phenomenon after the 1990s, the Jain community also developed in countries such as the USA, the UK, Belgium, Nepal, Thailand, and a few African countries. In this chapter, I present a detailed timeline of the arrival and spread of Jainism in North America.

When a Jain ascetic Vijayanand Suri, aka Muni Atmaram, was invited to participate in the first Parliament of World Religions in 1893 in Chicago, he refused to travel, thus honoring his ascetic vows but trained a young layman Virchand Gandhi, who became the first Jain to arrive in the USA. Virchand Gandhi accompanied the Hindu monk Swami Vivekananda and Brahmo Samaj leader Protap Chunder Mozoomdar to participate in the Parliament of World Religions in Chicago (Shah 2004, 55). While the 1900 US census had counted 2,050 Asian Indians (Okihiro 2001, 20), we have no way of knowing how many Jains were among them. With the resumption of Asian immigration with the 1965 law, the numbers of Jains also eventually continued to increase, especially as more Gujaratis, many of whom are Jains, took advantage of family-based immigration quotas (Dhingra 2012). Before this influx of Jains in America, at least one core principle of Jainism had already made its mark with the influence first of Mahatma Gandhi and then of Dr. Martin Luther King.

Virchand Gandhi and the arrival of Jainism in North America

At the time of the first Parliament of World's Religions in 1893, Jainism as a distinct religion was a recent discovery. Only in 1881 did the Census of India include the category of "Jain" for the first time (Flügel 2005). As noted above, Virchand R. Gandhi, a young lawyer of Bombay, was the only Jain at the first Parliament of World Religions in Chicago, held on September 11–27, 1893 (Hingrah and Dholakia-Dave 2012). In addition to talking about Jainism, he defended Indian culture against the missionary attacks during the parliament (Altman 2017). Following the parliament, Gandhi stayed on in the USA to lecture for two years. *The Buffalo Courier* reported that he was "accorded the greatest ovation ever granted to a speaker in Cassadaga," in the places where he was invited to speak during this time. He formed two organizations, *The School of Oriental Philosophy and Esoteric Studies*, under the supervision of William Pipe and the *Society for the Education of Women of India*, during his stay in the USA. During his second trip to USA and England in 1896-1897 (Jain 2011), Virchand Gandhi joined Charles C. Bonny, the President of the Parliament of World's Religions, to organize a Famine Relief Committee for India. This committee immediately sent about $10,000 and a steamer full of corns to India. During his two visits to the USA, he delivered more than 535 lectures on Jainism, yoga, Hindu culture, and Indian philosophy. *The New York Times* published an interview with him on November 29, 1897. His lectures were collected and published in four books, *Jain Philosophy* (1907), *Yoga Philosophy* (1912), *Karma Philosophy* (1913), and *The Systems of Indian Philosophy* (1970). Herbert Warren, who studied Jainism under him and adopted the Jain religion, published a book on his lectures entitled *Jainism*.

According to Kumar (1996a), the Howard family of Inglewood also adopted Jainism. Virchand Gandhi's speeches were well received, as shown by comments from that time. His colleague Swami Vivekananda said in a letter to Diwan, November 1894, "Now here is VRG, the Jain, whom you well know in Bombay. This man never takes anything but pure vegetables even in this cold climate, and tooth and nail tries to defend his countrymen and religion. The people of this country like him well." On October 3, 1893, *The Rochester Herald* published, "These lectures are instructive to both, old and young, and should be seen and heard all over America." Rev. R.A. White of Chicago said, "His lecture was a most scholarly production both in matter and form, and showed a thorough grasp of oriental philosophy." According to E.B. Sherman, of the U.S. Circuit Court, "It was rarely if ever, been my good fortune to meet a man whose reading and culture have been so wide and varied, and who, withal, has so sweet, sincere and teachable a spirit as Gandhi." Virchand Gandhi died on August 7, 1901, at the young age of 37, in India. Also in 1893, a Jain scholar named Shri Lalan came to the USA and stayed for more than four years. Inspired by his Jain teachings, an American woman, Ms. Howard, became a Jain practitioner and vegetarian[3].

American interest in Mahatma Gandhi and nonviolence

Americans had started hearing about Mahatma Gandhi in the 1920s when his noncooperation and nonviolent movement was challenging the British Raj in India. Mahatma Gandhi has continued to be a highly respected name in America since then. For instance, in 1921, John Haynes Holmes, a Unitarian minister, and an anti-war activist, told his congregation in New York (Rudolph 2010) that Mahatma Gandhi was "the greatest man in the world, greater even than Lenin and Woodrow Wilson. When I think of Mahatma Gandhi, I think of Jesus Christ." Another American theologian, Reinhold Niebuhr wrote very highly about Mahatma Gandhi and his nonviolence in his book, *Moral Man and Immoral Society* (1932):

> The advantage of non-violence as a method of expressing goodwill lies in the fact that it protects the agent against the resentments which violent conflict always creates in both parties to a conflict, and that it proves this freedom of resentment and ill will to the contending party in the dispute by enduring more suffering than it causes ... [O]ne of the most important results of a spiritual discipline against resentment in a social dispute is that it leads to an effort to discriminate between the evils of a social system and situation and the individuals who are involved in it ... Mr. Gandhi never tires of making a distinction between individual Englishmen and the system of imperialism which they maintain.

Time magazine put Gandhi on its cover page and declared "Saint Gandhi" to be "man of the year" for 1930[4] and "person of the century" in 1999.[5]

At least two prominent American journalists shaped popular opinion about Mahatma Gandhi and his nonviolent struggle against the British Raj by their reports. A widely influential American journalist Webb Miller, portrayed in the Hollywood film, *Gandhi* (1982), reported live as hundreds of Mahatma Gandhi's fellow nonviolent activists, *Satyagrahis*, were being beaten by the British police in 1930 during the Dharasana salt protest (cited in Sharma 2013),

> Bodies toppled over in threes and fours, bleeding from great gashes on their scalps. Group after group walked forward, sat down, and submitted to being beaten into insensibility without raising an arm to fend off the blows. Finally, the police became enraged by the non-resistance. They commenced savagely kicking the seated men in the abdomen and testicles. The injured men writhed and squealed in agony, which seemed to inflame the fury of the police. The police then began dragging the sitting men by the arms or feet, sometimes for a hundred yards, and throwing them into ditches.

A prominent photojournalist Margaret Bourke-White interviewed and photographed Mahatma Gandhi on January 30, 1948, before he was assassinated that same day, as also shown in the Hollywood biopic *Gandhi* (Bourke-White 1949, 225–233). However, even after Mahatma Gandhi passed away, he continued being relevant, especially during the Civil Rights Movement. Jainism's core ideal of nonviolence made its mark when Dr. Martin Luther King made it the pillar for his Civil Rights Movement, following in the footsteps of Mahatma Gandhi, who was in turn inspired by a Jain guru, Shrimad Rajchandra (King 1999; Helton 2007; Lakshmi 2009; Sharma 2013). Dr. King was introduced to Gandhi in Philadelphia, Pennsylvania, by Mordecai Johnson, the President of Howard University in Washington, DC, who had visited India earlier (Kennedy 2018, 28). Arguably, the most enduring image of Gandhian influence on America is perhaps the images of thousands of Civil Rights activists wearing the Gandhi white caps most notably during Dr. Martin Luther King's historic "I have a dream" speech in 1963 in Washington, DC.[6] The PBS film *This Far by Faith* mentions another Civil Rights Movement leader Dr. James Lawson who visited India to learn and experience Gandhian principles and nonviolent techniques.

> 1951, Reverend James Lawson was sentenced to three years in prison for refusing the Korean War draft. He was paroled after thirteen months, obtained his B.A. in 1952, and spent the next three years as a campus minister and teacher at Hislop College in Nagpur, India. While in India, Lawson eagerly read of the Montgomery Bus Boycott and the emerging nonviolent resistance movement back in the United States.[7] In Nashville, a brigade of students, many from seminary – were training for a nonviolent assault on segregation in their community. Their training was based on the teachings of Jesus and the principles of Mahatma Gandhi. Their leader was Rev. Lawson.[8]

Another Civil Rights leader who visited India was Bernard LaFayette (Kennedy 2018, 64), who was also inspired by Gandhi. Stephen Prothero went to the extent of calling the Civil Rights Movement an engagement with the Jain and Hindu philosophy of nonviolence in the film *The Asian & Abrahamic Religions: A Divine Encounter in America* by Krell et al. (2011). Also noted in the same documentary is the fact that 1968 was called the year of the guru by *Life* magazine.[9] Soon with the impetus provided by the Civil Rights Movement, immigration laws were changed and opened the floodgates for Asians, thus facilitating thousands of Jains to immigrate to the United States.

Chronological development of American Jainism

1900s

In 1904-1905, an artistic replica of the Jain temple of Palitana was sent by the British Government of India to the St. Louis Exposition World's Fair. This hand-carved teakwood temple's dimensions were 35 feet high, 20 square feet at base, and weighed 14 tons. After the Fair, the temple ended up at the Castaways Hotel in Las Vegas, Nevada and is now permanently installed at the Jain Center of Southern California in Los Angeles.

1919–1959

In 1919, Maurice Bloomfield, Professor of Sanskrit at Johns Hopkins University, published *Life and Stories of the 23rd Jain Tirthankara Parshvanath*, one of the first Jain texts to be published in North America. Champat Rai Jain, a lawyer from India, presented a talk, "Ahimsa as the Key to World Peace," at the World Fellowship of Faiths meeting in Chicago in 1933.

Available records show that in the early 1950s, a few North American people had adopted the Jain way of life. They were Wayne Steele of New York, Gary Benjamin of State University of Buffalo, Leona Smith Kremser of Oregon, Mark J. Kayda of Ohio, Alice Avery of California, May Fookes of Summerland, and James Brennan of Toronto (Kumar 1996a). During 1957–1959, Professor Archie J. Bahm, a philosopher at the University of New Mexico, had pioneered teaching courses on Jainism. His lectures were organized into sections such as introduction, metaphysics, epistemology, ethics, religion, and logic. In 1956, paintings by Ratu Shah depicting the dreams of Trishala, mother of Lord Mahavira, were included in *The Hungry Eye: An Introduction to Cosmic* Art, a book by Raymond F. Piper. In 1959, groups of Jains met in Michigan and New York.

The 1960s

In 1960, for the first time in North America, the anniversary of the birth of Lord Mahavira was celebrated and was broadcast on Voice of America Radio

International. Working with the American organization, Friends of Nonviolence, the Jains co-founded the Ahimsa Society in 1960. In the early 1960s, Narendra K. Sethi used to teach at Henry George School, where he introduced the basic tenets of Jainism into the courses. He also co-founded the India Centre with Rosalie Fennekohl, a millionaire social activist of New York. In 1960, this center conducted classes on Jainism and its literature, culture, and art on Friday evenings at the Indian Consulate office with the help of his mother Laxmidevi Sethi, a lay scholar of Jainism. This impetus gave rise to organizing one of the earliest seminars on Jainism at Columbia University. It was held on August 6, 1960, at Earl Hall on 116th St and Broadway. The keynote speaker, Arthur Cordts spoke on Jain philosophy while Marguerite Block of Columbia University gave a talk on the historicity of Jainism. Zigmund Cerbu, a scholar of Asian cultures and languages and an Assistant Professor of Religion at Columbia University, compared Jainism with Buddhism. Lay Jain scholars Wayne H. Steele, Narendra Sethi, and Lal Chand Jain, respectively, spoke on Jainism with themes such as the Jain literary contribution to other Indian languages and the Jain doctrine of Karma.

In 1966 and 1969, respectively, the first Jain Centers were established in New York City (called the Jain Center of America) and in Chicago. In 1970, Dhiraj Shah[10] succeeded in getting an exemption from being registered for military conscription by the Selective Service System. He used the Conscientious Objection, based on his religion of Jainism.

The 1970s

In 1971, Gurudev Chitrabhanu was the first Jain monk to visit the USA (Long 2009, 79) at the invitation of Harvard Divinity School.[11] Later, he returned to the USA and left the traditional monkhood. In 1975, Gurudev started the Jain Meditation International Center in New York City and offered classes on reverence for life, Jain philosophy, yoga, meditation, and vegetarianism. In 1973, the Jain Center of Greater Boston was established (under the leadership of Sulekh Jain) with several ground-breaking projects, such as publishing the *Jain Study Circular* in 1979 (edited by Duli Chand Jain) that used to be mailed for free across North America. It also created the first directory of Jains in North America in 1979. In 1981, the center developed its temple from a former Swedish Lutheran church in suburban Norwood. In 1973, the Jain Society of Toronto was established. In 1975, the Jain Center of Northern California was established and the second Jain monk, Sushil Muni, visited the USA. He was the first Jain monk to travel abroad and continued his ascetic life, unlike Gurudev Chitrabhanu. In 1978, Sushil Yogaville was established in Burlington Flats, New York, and the land and the building for it was donated to Sushil Muni by a Russian lady. In 1978–1979, he founded the first Jain Ashram in Burlington Flats near Utica in New York. He also founded the first Jain center of pilgrimage known as Siddhachalam in New Jersey in 1983. Sushil Muni passed away on April 22, 1994, at the age of 68, after providing crucial leadership to American Jains for almost two decades.

In 1975, the Jain Society of Greater Detroit began with 50 families and, as of 2019, has grown to over 600 families. This society holds a Jain study class for more than 150 children, sponsors lectures by visiting scholars, and celebrates Jain festivals. It marks Thanksgiving Day as the Ahimsa Day, a day of nonviolence. Its temple in Farmington Hills, a Detroit suburb, opened in 1998. The temple organizes periodic charity activities such as donating food, clothes and other items to homeless people in Oakland County, donating medical equipment to third world countries, and supporting an animal sanctuary. It also supports the Lighthouse Center that was founded by one of the disciples of Gurudev Chitrabhanu for the practice of Jain way of life.

In 1976, the Jain Center of Rochester, New York, was established. The Kundalini Science Center, founded by Sushil Muni, was incorporated in Chicago. In 1978, the Jain Society of Greater Cleveland, Ohio, was formed. The Society was instrumental in the establishment of Siddhachalam in 1983. The Mayor of Cleveland proclaimed April 26, 1981, as a Day of Ahimsa (nonviolence) in Cleveland. Also in 1978, Pat Bruno adopted the name Swami Padmananda as she was initiated as a householder Jain by Sushil Muni.[12]

In 1979, Sushil Muni Jain Ashram was established in Staten Island, New York. Also, in that year, Chetana Catherine Florida, one of the first disciples of Gurudev Chitrabhanu, established the Lighthouse Center in Michigan to conduct various activities inspired by the Jain philosophy, as mentioned earlier. She met Gurudev Chitrabhanu in the 1980s who initiated her as his disciple in Palitana, India, with a new spiritual name Chetana (literally, awareness). According to Pramodaji, Gurudev's wife, to become a Jain, first, the person had to be ready and convinced about being initiated into Jain Dharma. They were asked to become vegetarian first and memorize Namokar Mantra. On the day of their initiation, they were blessed with *vāskhep* (sacred sandalwood powder) and their right wrists were tied with *Raksha Potli* (a sacred bracelet). They were then given the Indian names after feeling their vibrations. There was no particular day, but whenever they were ready to surrender to the Tirthankar became the day for their initiation (Chetana 2006).

In 1979, Professor Padmanabh S. Jaini published *The Jaina Path of Purification*, a distinguished academic contribution to the understanding of Jainism in the West. Also in 1979, *Jainism*, an introductory book by Ramnik V. Shah (Vividus) was published by Carlton Press, New York. In 1979, the Jain Center of Greater Boston released the first edition of the *Jain Directory of North America*. Also in that year, the Jain Center of Southern California and the Jain Study Center of North Carolina were established, that have conducted various study activities.

1980–1981

With the sizable number of Jain immigrants from India, in 1981, in Los Angeles, JAINA, the Federation of Jain Associations in North America, was founded, inspired by the two Jain gurus, Chitrabhanu and Sushil Muni. As of

2019, more than 70 Jain organizations across North America are affiliated with JAINA, including Jain temples, societies, and centers. More than 110 directors of such local and regional Jain centers elect the JAINA Executive Committee and 30 other working committees biannually. JAINA publishes a quarterly magazine, called *Jain Digest* and its headquarters is in California. JAINA regularly participates at major interfaith events, such as the Parliament of World Religions.

In 1980, the International Mahavir Jain Mission (IMJM) was founded in Cleveland, Ohio, with Sushil Muni as the chairperson and Tansukh Salgia as its President. Also in 1980, the Jain Center of Connecticut, the Jain Society of Metropolitan Washington, the Jain Sangha of New Jersey (Cherry Hill), and the Jain Meditation Center of Toronto were established.

In 1981, the first International Jain Conference was organized at the UN Plaza in New York City under the leadership of Sushil Muni. Also in 1981, the Jain Group of Atlanta was established. In 1981, Sulekh Jain, who had co-founded the Jain Center in Boston in 1973, led the efforts to develop the Jain Society in Ohio and served as the founding president till 1984. Also in the early 1980s, the Jain Society of Cincinnati and Dayton was established.

In line with American Hindu temples (Narayanan 2007), the non-sectarian Jain temples prevalent in North America, where Jains of all different sects come to pray, is a unique phenomenon that has not been taken up in India. While some still hold to the sectarian views, most of the Jains born in North America have remained non-sectarians (Mehta, 2017). In North America, JAINA and all the dozens of Jain temples that are affiliated with it, have successfully kept this ecumenical focus in all their activities despite some sectarian tendencies within American Jainism, such as the International Digamber Jain Organization and Guru-led movements, e.g., Shrimad Rajchandra Mission. Also, even the non-sectarian temples deal with different sects in ways such as keeping the Śvetāmbara and Digambara statues in two separate temple rooms, teaching children both versions of rituals, and alternating sectarian practice at festivals, such as Paryushana.

As mentioned earlier, this revolutionary institution was the dream of two visionaries, Sushil Muni and Gurudev Chitrabhanu. JAINA continues to publish standard Pathshala books for children, an annual JAINA calendar, the quarterly magazine, *Jain Digest*, and organizes unified pilgrimages to both Śvetāmbara and Digambara temples in India. Most North American Jain temples cater to the spiritual needs of Jains of all sects. Indian scholars and monks of all Jain sects visit most of these centers periodically. Similarly, Jains of all denominations from across North America participate in JAINA's biannual national conventions held in different cities. The two Jain youth organizations for students and professionals, Young Jains of America and Young Jain Professionals, respectively, also function in a similar ecumenical spirit. JAINA and these affiliated youth organizations have inspired Jains in India, the UK, Kenya, and elsewhere to unite under an ecumenical umbrella but such efforts there have not yet completely succeeded. Lalit Shah, one of the co-founders of the Jain Center of Southern California, talked to many Jains around the country about organizing a convention over the Memorial Day weekend in 1981. At the same time, Sushil Muni was talking with Tansukh Salgia in Ohio and many other people about the need for a unifying organization of all Jains. When Lalit Shah spoke to Salgia, they agreed to meet in Los Angeles in May of 1981. The four Jain centers of Washington, DC, Cleveland, Northern California, and Southern California officially participated, but there were many participants from other centers as well. Both Gurudev Chitrabhanu and Sushil Muni co-led that two-day effort. Professor Padmanabh Jaini was the invited scholar for the first meeting, and Lalit Shah was named as the President of this new organization for the next two years. Tansukh Salgia brought with him a draft constitution that was revised and accepted as an ad hoc constitution. The name of the organization at the time was the Federation of Jain Organizations of North America. All the participants agreed to meet again in New York in two years to ratify the constitution and formalize the organization. After the convention in Los Angeles, Lalit Shah and Sushil Muni went to Las Vegas to look at a wooden replica of the Palitana Temple. This replica had been sent to the St. Louis World Fair by the British Government in 1904, as noted earlier. After some challenges and problems, the temple was finally acquired and has been put on display at the Jain Center of Southern California in Los Angeles. Also, in 1981, Clare Rosenfield published a book, *Gurudev Shree Chitrabhanu: A Man with a Vision* and included an interview with Chitrabhanu and some of his writings and discourses. It was published by the Jain Meditation International Center of New York.

1982

In 1982, the Jain Society of Houston and of North Texas were established. In 1988, Jains in North Texas purchased a former Christian church and transformed it into a Jain Center. In 1993, the Jain Society of North Texas celebrated their temple Pratishtha Mahotsav sanctification ceremony for the image of Lord Mahavira, Lord Parshvanath, and a marble carving of Namokar Mantra. This North Texan temple is one of the earliest temples that followed the new format acceptable to all sects as defined by JAINA. Gurudev Chitrabhanu and Bhattarak Charukeerthi blessed the occasion. In 2012, they purchased the BAPS Hindu temple and transformed it into a Jain temple. The society has more than 400 members and more than 300 students in the Sunday Pathshala as of 2019, making it the fifth largest Jain Sunday School in the nation.[13] The temple also facilitates and sponsors regular annual visits by several scholars and ascetics. They also own the 5.6-acre land in another suburb, Garland, on which *Charan Paduka* (divine footprint) was installed in December 2011 as a symbolic extension of the temple. More details of this temple are available in Appendix 3. Also in 1982, the Jain Society of New Jersey was inaugurated in a former church that was eventually converted into a Jain temple by installing three marble images of the Tirthankaras, fordmakers, that were brought from India.[14]

Similarly, in 1983, the Jain Society of Boston turned a church into a Jain temple. Also in 1983, Siddhachalam was established in New Jersey by Sushil Muni. This 108-acre rural temple complex is a residential community for Jain ascetics. Jain lay people also stay here for spiritual retreats. In 1983, the Jain Study Group of Charlotte, North Carolina was established.

The second JAINA Convention was held in New York in 1983 with the participation of approximately 200 people. After much debate, a constitution was adopted there. The name of the organization was changed to the Federation of Jain Associations in North America (JAINA). Representatives of 11 centers signed the new constitution. Manoj Dharmsi was elected as the president. In December of 1985, the IRS recognized JAINA as a 501 (c)(3) tax-exempt organization. In 1992, JAINA was registered as a non-profit corporation in the State of Virginia. Manoj Dharamsi made the initial attempts to encourage more centers to join the federation. Soon, all 15 of the largest centers of those days had joined the federation, and today, more than 70 centers in the USA and Canada have become members of JAINA. The objectives of JAINA are the following:[15]

1 Promote religious and educational activities related to Jain religion and develop a better understanding of the Jain religion.
2 Assist and promote charitable and humanitarian activities in North America and worldwide.
3 Actively promote vegetarianism and nonviolence.
4 Provide and promote academic and cultural exchanges among Jains everywhere.
5 Assist existing Jain associations and support the formation of new Jain associations in North America.
6 Serve as a liaison with government agencies in pursuance of the above objectives.
7 Foster cordial relationships with interfaith or multi-faith organizations.

1984

In 1984, JAINA arranged for Hukamchand Bharill, Pratapkumar Tolia, Prem Suman Jain, and V. P. Jain to visit various centers. Thus, the Scholar Visitation Program of JAINA was born. As of 2019, the JAINA roster has grown to more than 100 visiting scholars and monks. In 1984, a children's religious book was prepared which had five sections: stories, sutras, mantras, philosophy, and hymns.[16] JAINA has distributed books and recordings of scholarly lectures. Since 1988, it has celebrated Paryushana and Das Lakshana Parva together uniting all Jains of different sects. Starting in 1992, it has observed the first Sunday of October as Ahimsa Day and has distributed food and clothing to the needy and homeless people in their city. It has supported several relief and animal compassion activities in India as well as in North America by donating money, food, and clothes to various agencies. It has also organized an annual Jain camp for adults and children to conduct yoga, meditation, and religious discourses.

1985

The Jain Society of Greater Detroit agreed to host the third JAINA Convention during the Memorial Day weekend of 1985. At that gathering, several goals were identified: strengthening of the Scholar Visitation Program; publishing a youth directory; and arranging youth programs; publishing a quarterly news magazine; and supporting the publication of Jain literature. Around 250 people attended that convention. Tansukh Salgia was elected the President, and he served two terms of two years each. During his Presidency, JAINA supported Michael Tobias in making his documentary *Ahimsa* (nonviolence) that was shown on PBS. JAINA membership during those four years grew to about 30 centers. He also formalized periodic Executive Committee meetings. The JAINA library was started with the help of Prem Gada, Professor Malukchand Shah of Ahmedabad, and Sulekh Jain. Initially, the library was housed at the Jain Center of West Texas in Lubbock. In 2000, it was moved to the Jain Center of Southern California, and today the library has grown to over 10,000 volumes.

S. A. Bhuvanendra Kumar of the Jain Society of Toronto was named the editor of JAINA's quarterly publication, *Jain Digest*. In August of 1985, the first issue of *Jain Digest* was published. This marked a crucial point in the development and growth of JAINA. The publication raised funds through a *Jain Digest* patron program with a donation of $101.00, matrimonial announcements, sponsorship of issues by individuals, and advertisements. Over the years, *Jain Digest* has become an essential part of JAINA by reporting news and events of JAINA. Issues originally were typed by hand, and about 500 copies were printed that were mailed to all the Jain centers in the USA. In 1989, after Sulekh Jain became JAINA's president, over 7,000 Jain homes started received *Jain Digest*, the quarterly publication covering Jain news worldwide. The expanded mailing was made possible by the generous donation by Pramod Jhaveri of the Jain Center of Cincinnati and Dayton, as the editor S. A. B. Kumar laboriously had produced *Jain Digest* on a shoestring budget. Circulation reached over 5,000 copies, and more importantly, the magazine became a well-respected Jain magazine in many parts of the world. The initial commitment of free distribution to every known Jain family in North America has been preserved to this date when more than 10,000 homes continue to receive it for free.

In 1985, the Assembly of World Religions sponsored by the International Religious Foundation was held at McAfee, NJ. Sushil Muni represented Jain religion at the assembly. Also in 1985, the Jain Center of Phoenix, the Jain Social Group of Los Angeles, the Jain Center of Syracuse, and IMJM of Ontario were established under the spiritual guidance of Sushil Muni and Gurudev Chitrabhanu. IMJM had organized the first Jain Arhum Yoga Camp for youths for a week in 1985 and continued this activity every year. In 1986, the Jain Center of Greater St. Louis was established.

1986

In 1986, Siddha Chakra Puja, comprising of more than 25 different rituals for Arihanta, Siddha, Acharya, Upadhyay, Sadhu, Darshan, Jnan, Charitra, and Tapa, were performed at several places in North America for the first time. In 1986, in Washington, DC, Navin and Leela Shah served 400 homeless persons an Indian vegetarian meal on the anniversary of the birth of Lord Mahavira. Also in the same year, the New York public library organized the first exhibition of Jain paintings from May 23 to September 20, 1986. The exhibition was entitled "The World of Jainism." The exhibits included images from the fifteenth to the nineteenth century depicting the *Kalpa Sutra* and other Jain texts. These little-known Jain manuscripts were from the Spencer Collection.

In September 1986, the World Jain Congress was convened at Siddhachalam, New Jersey. The theme of the conference was Jain Unity, and about 1,200 people attended it from North America, Europe, Africa, and India. Also in 1986, the Jain Community of Buffalo, the Jain Association of Montreal, and the Lord Mahavira mini-temple were established in Raleigh, North Carolina.

In 1987, the second edition of the *Jain Directory of North America* was issued by the Jain Center of Greater Boston. In 1987, Sushil Muni's book, *Song of the Soul*, was published by Siddhachalam publishers of New Jersey. Also, in the same year, the Ohio state governor Richard F. Celeste honored Mohan Bafna and Tansukh Salgia with the Governor's Special Recognition Award. The fourth JAINA Convention was held in Chicago. Earlier the Jain Society of Metropolitan Chicago had bought 15 acres of land for an ambitious temple project at an estimated cost of $1 million. Michael Tobias' PBS documentary, *Ahimsa*, was supported by JAINA and was shown to the 700 attendees at the convention. Gurudev Chitrabhanu, Devendrakirti Bhattarak, Laxmisena Bhattarak, and Hukamchand Bharil were the prominent speakers. This year also marked the ground-breaking ceremonies for the Jain Center of Southern California, and Siddhachalam took place. The temple in southern California was the first Jain Temple in North America built from the ground up. In 1987, Dulichand Jain started the Jain Study Circle. Its newsletter, *Jain Study Circular*, previously published by the Jain Center of Boston, published articles on Jain philosophy and practice.

In 1987, the first Jain documentary, *Ahimsa*, was released on the PBS. Professor Padmanabh S. Jaini of the University of California Berkeley was the script consultant. Sushil Muni and Gurudev Chitrabhanu, prominent spiritual leaders, were among those interviewed in the film. In 1987, the Scholar Visitation Program Committee was established by JAINA under the leadership of Tansukh Salgia. The mission of the committee is to sponsor, support, and organize the programs at various Jain centers of North America for Jain monks, nuns, and scholars of India and around the world. It organizes the programs for 10–15 scholars every year. Since 1987, the committee has organized the programs for Jain monks, such as Triputi Bandhu, Rupchand,

and Manak Muni, nuns, such as Chandana and Madhusmita, Bhattaraks such as Charukeerthi, Devendrakeerti, scholars such as Hukamchand Bharill, Pratap Tolia, Kumarpal Desai, N. P. Jain, Dhirajlal Mehta, Nareshbhai Doshi, Sagarmal Jain, Dinesh Modi, Shashikant Mehta, Jitendra Shah, Rajendra Kamdar, and many more.

1988

In 1988, Jain temples opened in Los Angeles and Dallas. Also in 1988, unity of Paryushana (for the Śvetāmbara sect) and Daslakshana (Digambara) Parva was advocated by the Jain Study Center of North Carolina (Raleigh). Both festivals are now celebrated together across North America on evenings and weekends.

1989

In 1989, the Jain Society of Rochester organized a forum for young Jains. Both the Jain Society of Metropolitan Washington and the Jain Society of Greater Detroit bought land to build temples, and the Jain Sangh of South Jersey purchased a building to convert it into a temple. The image of Lord Mahavir was installed at the Hindu Jain Cultural Center Edmonton, Canada. JAINA sponsored visits by a group of three Jain monks known as Triputi Bandhu. That year, the 5th JAINA Convention was held in Toronto from July 1–.Since then, the convention dates have been permanently changed to the long weekend in July to synchronize with US-Canadian holidays and encourage the participation of children during the summer school holidays. Attendance at this convention of 2,000 set a new record for JAINA. At this convention, Sulekh Jain was elected President of JAINA for a two-year term. Dulichand Jain of New York, the editor of *Jain Study Circular*, was presented with the inaugural JAINA Ratna Award, the highest Jain recognition in North America, in recognition of his contributions through his writings and scholarship. A new feature, an exhibition of Jain paintings was introduced at this convention. Later in that year, the Marriage Information Service of JAINA was launched under the leadership of Fakirchand Dalal of Maryland. Monks, Bhattaraks, scholars, Jain leaders, and other dignitaries, namely, Sushil Muni, Gurudev Chitrabhanu, Jain monks Triputi Bandhu (three brother monks), Bhattarak Charukeerthi, Dinesh Modi, and Bruce Costain (aka Balabhadra) attended the convention. Jains from various countries, namely, India, England, Germany, and Zambia, participated in the conference.

In 1989, when Surendra K. Jain became the editor of *Jain Digest*, he made significant changes in its format. First, he changed it to a regular 8½ x 11 paper size, doubling the available space. All the issues now were computer set with graphics and photographs. In addition to general articles, five regular sections were introduced: national and international news, calendar, education and library, matrimonial service, and youth corner. A table of contents was added, and the more readable font was used. An executive advisory board was set up, and the inside cover started to list all the officers of JAINA. New regular features also included extensive book reviews and letters to the editors. *Jain Digest* today has retained that format, but now the inside pages have color, and coated stock is used.

In 1989, Urmila Talsania and others launched the Young Jains of America, an organization exclusively for youth. Also, in 1989, the Jain Society of Southern Florida was established. Also in that year, the Brahmi Jain Society was founded to promote academic research in Jainism. It also launched a new quarterly journal *Jinamanjari* that was distributed for free to more than 250 educational institutions in the USA, Canada, and India. Its chief editor was Bhuvanendra Kumar in Canada, and Tansukh Salgia was the President of Brahmi Jain Society. Also, in 1989, the anniversary of the birth of Lord Mahavira was celebrated by the Unitarian Universalist Church of Racine, Wisconsin. The program consisted of Namokar Mantra chanting, reading of Jain scriptures, the anointment of Lord Mahavira, making swastikas with rice, and discourse on Jain respect for life. They were able to install the image of Lord Mahavira. In the same year, the Hindu temple at Edmonton, Canada, installed the image of Lord Mahavira. Also in the same year, Jain centers were established in Minnesota, Alberta in Canada, and Silver Spring, Maryland.

In July 1989, the Center for the Study of World Religions at Harvard University hosted a Jainism and Ecology Conference. This conference was sponsored and funded by the Jain Academic Foundation of North America (JAFNA). Nine scholars from the USA, Canada, and the UK presented their research to 22 participants of the workshop. In 1990, *India Abroad*, a New York-based newspaper, devoted three full pages to the Jain community. The article included Delhi's three-story hospital for birds, the development of Jainism in North America, and Jain demographic information.

1990

In 1990, the Jain Society built a new Jain temple in Toronto. By 1990, the JAINA library was fully operational with over 4,000 books in English, Gujarati, and Hindi and was managed by Premchand Gada in Lubbock and later in Dallas, Texas. Many books from this library were gifted to the University of North Texas and elsewhere. This was also the year when two Terapanthi nuns, Smit Prajna, and Akshaya Prajna, made their first visit to the USA.[17] They visited Jain centers in New Jersey, Toronto, Raleigh, Atlanta, and New York. At each center, they gave a brief introduction to Preksha Dhyana and lectured on the principles of Jainism. That year Nathmal Tatia, Director of Jain Vishwa Bharati in Ladnun, was a visiting Professor at Harvard University. Tatia was invited to speak by many Jain centers. That same year the Jain Center of Boston began the task of revising the North American *Jain Directory*.

In October 1990, a delegation of nine prominent Jains led by President Sulekh Jain, representing various Jain centers in the USA and Canada joined other Jain leaders from the UK, France, Belgium, India, Kenya and Singapore on a visit to the Buckingham Palace in London to meet with H.R.H. Prince Philip. There they discussed the Jain Declaration on Nature written by Ambassador L. M. Singhvi. The meeting opened with recitals of the Namokar Mantra and this was probably the first time this had occurred at the palace, and ended with Khame Mi Savva Jiva. After a lengthy exchange of views, Prince Philip showed appreciation for the Jain Community's efforts and Jainism's stand on nature and preservation of the environment. A Jain Sacred Literature Trust was formed as part of International Sacred Literature Trust, supported by H.R.H. Prince Philip. This international gathering of Jains was well received and given a civic reception by the Lord and Lady Mayor of the city of Leicester. The entire event was well covered in the media in India, the UK, and the USA.

The JAINA Executive Committee met in St. Louis, Missouri, in November 1990 where two committees were formed to conduct the elections and present the awards. The award committee was charged with recognition of individuals for their contributions in the promotion of Jainism in North America. A delegation from the Jain Center of Northern California briefed the committee on preparations for the 1991 convention. Also in 1990, a Jain student Neal Shah, attending a Catholic high school in Buffalo, New York, was permitted to study Jainism for his religious studies requirement.[18] It was arranged as an independent study, and the teacher was given a set of books on Jainism. In the same year, the Jain Sangha of Tri-State celebrated the opening of a new Jain temple at Pennsauken, New Jersey. The celebration lasted for three days and throughout the festivities, Jain philosophy lectures, cultural programs, and various pujas, devotional songs, chanting, were performed by multiple groups. More than 2,200 people attended the ceremony daily.

The year 1990 also saw Gurudev Chitrabhanu as a keynote speaker at the Vegetarian World Conference in Tel Aviv, Israel, and the Jain Society of Toronto and International Mahavir Jain Mission of Canada organized Jain philosophy and religion broadcasts on television for 13 weeks. Also, the Kachchi Oswal Jain Community held its first convention from September 1–3, 1990, at Siddhachalam, New Jersey. More than 700 Jains from the USA, Canada, and India attended the three-day gathering.

1991

The Jain Center of Central Ohio was established in Columbus, and a workshop exploring the pluralism of religions was held at Harvard University in October 1991. JAINA actively participated in the meeting. The Sixth Biennial JAINA convention was held and hosted by the Jain Center of Northern California. This convention achieved a significant milestone in the history of the JAINA Conventions. It catapulted the meeting into a national Jain conference, an event attended by all Jains, young and old. About 3,000 people, including 500 youth, participated in the convention. The venue for the meeting was Stanford University and was organized around the theme "Extending Jain Heritage to the Next Generation." The main speakers at the conference included Acharya Sushil Muni, Gurudev Chitrabhanu, N. P. Jain, L. M. Singhvi, Gov. Jerry Brown, Professor Padmanabh Jaini, Professor John Cort, Michael Tobias, and Lt. Gov. Leo McCarthy of California. The convention was organized into many parallel tracks with sessions and panel discussions on Jain philosophy, literature, and art. The speakers included a mix of religious leaders as well as academics from major universities. Sulekh Jain was re-elected as JAINA President for the second two-year term, and Prem Gada was given the JAINA Ratna award. Also, JAINA declared the first Sunday of October as the Ahimsa Day (a day of nonviolence) celebrating the birth week of Mahatma Gandhi.

Jains in North America were the host to 19 British Jain youth (under the leadership of Atul Shah from the UK) who visited New York, San Francisco, Los Angeles, Washington, Buffalo, Toronto, and the JAINA convention at Stanford University. The UK Jain youth presented a variety show comprising two plays, dances, and slide show at all the Jain centers.

Also, in 1991, thousands of Jains participated in a grand ritual inaugural ceremony at Siddhachalam, New Jersey, to establish the new images of the Jain Tirthankaras, Adinath, Parshvanath, Chandraprabha, Mahavira, and others. The event, *Pratishtha Mahotsav*, was led by Sushil Muni, the founder of Siddhachalam. In 1991, the book, *Gender and Salvation*, was published by Professor Padmanabh S. Jaini at the University of California at Berkeley. Michael Tobias published another book, *Life Force: The World of Jainism*. The International Alumni Association of Mahavir Jain Vidyalaya was established to support Jain students and support Mahavir Jain School and other Jain educational institutions in India. The Association received a donation of $200,000 in two years. They also supported a higher education institution for girls in India. In 1991, the Jain Social Group of Toronto was established, and the Hindu Temple Society installed Lord Mahavira's image in Augusta, GA, under the guidance of Sushil Muni on September 28, 1991. The JAINA Education Conference took place in New York in December 1991 with more than 40 teachers and scholars from across North America. The aim of the conference was to establish a standard Jain curriculum to teach Jainism to Jain youth. Prem Gada organized this conference. Also, in 1991, Pravin K. Shah, from Raleigh, North Carolina, launched a 12-hour course on Jainism for youth.

1992

In December 1992, the Speaker of the Indian Parliament, Shivraj Patil honored JAINA in New Delhi. IMJM was recognized as a non-governmental organization by the United Nations. Meanwhile, the Jain Center of Greater Boston published the third edition of the *Jain Directory* on the anniversary of the birth of Lord Mahavira. The directory included information on more than 5,000 Jain families living in North America. It also contained various statistics on the Jain community. Also, in 1992, Pravin K. Shah launched the Jain Education and Information Electronic Bulletin Board System.[19] Sushil Muni represented American Jains at the UN Earth Summit in Rio de Janeiro, the Animal Compassion and Vegetarianism Committee was established within JAINA, the first four-month rainy season retreat (*chaturmas*) was organized in California for two Terapanthi Jain monks. During this period, two Jain ascetics (*Saman*s Shrut Prajna and Ashwin Prajna) gave lectures on Preksha meditation.

1993

In 1993, the Jain Society of Metropolitan Chicago constructed a new temple with Digambara and Śvetāmbara Jain Tirthankara images and the Shrimad Rajchandra's Swadhyaya Hall. Also in that year, Albany celebrated Pratishtha Mahotsav for the image of Lord Mahavira in the Hindu Temple on May 29–30, 1993. Sushil Muni, Gurudev Chitrabhanu, Vijay Muni, Dinesh Muni, and Padmaprabha Muni blessed the occasion. Also in 1993, the centennial celebration of the Parliament of World Religions was held from August 28 to September 5, 1993, in Chicago, with JAINA being the co-sponsor of the event. More than 30 Jain scholars from the USA, India, England, and Africa presented 42 papers. More than 300 Jains of different sects from all over the world attended the conference. Also in 1993, JAINA participated in Mahamastakabhisheka celebration of Lord Bahubali in Karnataka, India. An international group of Jains, including representatives of JAINA, participated in Mahamastakabhisheka celebration of Lord Bahubali at Shravanabelgola, India.

The seventh biennial JAINA Convention was held in Pittsburgh with more than 5,000 people. Jagat Jain was elected President of JAINA and Dhiraj Shah was awarded the JAINA Ratna award. An exhibition of more than 400 masterpieces of art and literature collected from the National Museum of India, the American Institute of Indian Studies, Bharatiya Jnanpith, and the Jaibhikhhu Trust was displayed. Also in 1993, JAINA was invited to the White House. The occasion was the signing of the Religious Freedom Restoration Act (HR 1308) by President Clinton. Amrender Muni, Naresh Jain, Arvind Vora, Peter Bheda, Harshad Lakhani, and Dhiraj Shah attended this prestigious ceremony in the Rose Garden of the White House. The aim of the Act was to guarantee the rights of minorities to build their temples or other houses of prayers. In June 1993, the Jain Society of Metropolitan Chicago held the Pratishtha for their temple. Also at the 1993 convention, JAINA's Animal Compassion and Vegetarianism Committee presented on vegetarianism and veganism. This event marked the beginning of collaborations between this committee and other vegetarian and animal rights groups, such as the American Vegan Society, the Vegetarian Resource Group, and PETA (People for the Ethical Treatment of Animals).

In 1993, Bharat Shah published *An Introduction to Jainism*. The Jain Center of British Columbia was established although the organization had been founded in 1984. By the end of 1993, JAINA's membership had grown from 29 in 1989 to 49 Jain Centers. Among several initiatives, the JAINA Executive Committee started meeting every quarter at a member Jain center. After the Paryushan, the JAINA Executive Committee met regularly at Siddhachalam. During 1991 and 1993, JAINA established a World Community Service and created a fund to help communities across the world who were devastated by natural disasters. This fund has helped build houses and schools in India, Haiti, and other places. The JAINA constitution that was adopted in 1983 was revised with minor changes in 1985, 1988, and in 1992.

1994

In 1994, significant constitutional changes were made, creating six regional Vice President Positions in the JAINA Executive Committee and a new system of the election of officers by mail was introduced. The switch to mail ballots enabled higher participation by JAINA directors in the election process. Also in 1994, the first convention of Young Jains of America (YJA) was organized for three days in Chicago with about 430 Jain youth participants. Also in that year, JAINA's Animal Compassion and Vegetarianism Committee held a workshop, in Los Angeles, in which 15 young Jains made presentations based on vegetarianism and veganism. A booklet summarizing the workshop proceedings, *Ahimsa Beyond Vegetarianism*, was also published.

1995–1996

In 1995, Narendra Sheth of this Committee held similar workshops in Houston, Austin, Lubbock, Dallas, Cincinnati, Detroit, and finally in Chicago at the 1995 JAINA Convention. Also in that year, Michael Tobias published *A Naked Man*, a novel dramatizing the mission of peace in the footsteps of Lord Mahavira. Also, the *Essence of World Religions* book was compiled by Pravin K. Shah of Raleigh, NC, and published by the Jain Study Center of NC.

In the same year, Los Angeles County of Museum of Art organized the Jain exhibition known as "The Peaceful Liberators: Jain Art from India." The museum opened in Los Angeles from November 1994 to January 1995. Later, it moved to Kimbell Art Museum in Fort Worth, Texas, and then to New Orleans Museum of Art. Approximately 800,000 people saw this most extensive collection of Jain artwork and cultural programs and presentations during the exhibitions.

In 1995, the book, *The Wave of Bliss: Impact of Chitrabhanu on the Western World*, was compiled by N. P. Jain, former ambassador to United Nations. The book was based on hundreds of letters written to Gurudev Chitrabhanu by his non-Indian followers. In 1995, the Jain Center was founded in Portland, Oregon. Also in 1995, Manubhai Doshi's two books were published: *Prabhavana:*

Essence of Jainism and *Samayika: Journey towards Peace and Tranquility.* Also in that year, JAINA's Animal Compassion and Vegetarianism Committee participated at the Vegan Festival in San Diego, California. Members of the local Jain community performed plays depicting the compassionate Jain stories of Abhaya Kumar and Nem-Rajul. Chicago was once again the host of the JAINA convention in 1995. It attracted the highest number of delegates to date, 9,000. Manilal Mehta was elected President, and Manoj Dharamsi was presented with the JAINA Ratna award. Pratishtha Mahotsav of the Jain Society of Houston was performed in November of 1995. In April of 1996, the Jain Society of Alberta in Edmonton, Canada, celebrated the Pratishtha Mahotsav of their temple.

1997

The Jain Society of Toronto hosted the 1997 JAINA Convention. Dhiraj Shah was elected as the President and Tansukh Salgia was presented with the JAINA Ratna award. In September 1997, JAINA was invited to meet Prime Minister Vajpayee at the Waldorf Astoria Hotel. Dhiraj Shah submitted a memorandum with requests, such as financial allocation for the 2600th anniversary of the birth of Lord Mahavir and a commemorative stamp in honor of Virchand Raghavchand Gandhi. The government of India subsequently honored many of these requests. Manubhai Doshi's book, *Spiritual Code and Restraints: Heart of Jain Practice* was published in this year.

1999

Mahendra Pandya was elected the President at the 1999 JAINA convention, held in Philadelphia. Here, a *Chaumukha* (with four façades) temple was displayed by Nipul Shah of San Jose, California. This began the tradition of creating temples at each of the following conventions. Pravin K. Shah received the JAINA Ratna award that year. In the same year, Atul Shah of the UK launched a new magazine, *Jain Spirit*, with support from Jains in North America. In 1999, JAINA representatives, including N. P. Jain, Amrender Muni, and Kumarpal Desai, presented several papers at the third Parliament of World Religions in Cape Town, South Africa.

2001

In 2001, the Jain Society of Metropolitan Chicago hosted the JAINA convention. Bipin Parikh became the President, and the JAINA Ratna Award was presented to Manibhai Mehta. Mehta was profiled by the *Los Angeles Times* (Loar 1996). In 2001, for the first time, a Jain prayer was recited at the opening session of the US House of Representatives by Gurudev Chitrabhanu. Also for the first time, a Jain prayer for peace was recited by Samani Akshaya Pragya and Sanmati Pragya at the opening of the Ohio Senate on

September 18, 2001. Tansukh Salgia organized it in cooperation with the Jain Center of Central Ohio.

2002–2003

Vinay Jain and his wife, Kanika Jain, founded the Jiv Daya Foundation in 2002 with the mission of improving the quality of life of people around the world. Cincinnati was the venue for the 2003 JAINA convention. Anop Vora was elected President, and Arvind Vora received the JAINA Ratna Award. The Cincinnati convention generated a respectable financial surplus for JAINA. During Anop Vora's Presidency, JAINA revamped the website and began publishing the electronic newsletter. This newsletter propelled JAINA into the electronic age and provided a dynamic tool to bring JAINA closer to its constituents.

2004

In 2004, JAINA led the Unified Jain Delegation of Jain scholars, monks, youth and volunteers from India, the UK, Africa, and North America to the Parliament of World Religions in Barcelona, Spain. Additionally, JAINA allocated a significant budget for the distribution of flyers on Jainism and JAINA.

2009

In 2009, a weekly TV show *Mangalam* was launched for news and interviews with Jain scholars. A free website JainLibrary.org was launched, which is the most extensive collection of more than 20,000 files containing Jain books, manuscripts, audio recordings, articles, and magazines in Gujarati, Hindi, English, Prakrit, Sanskrit, and other languages. As of 2019, it has more than 51,000 registered users from across the world. In 2009–2010, JAINA and other Jain organizations from the UK and Africa co-sponsored a Mobility Camp in Palitana, India, to benefit more than 25,000 disabled people. Also, in 2009, Sulekh Jain was awarded the JAINA Ratna Award. He became the ninth winner as of 2019.

The biennial JAINA conventions were held respectively in 2005 in San Francisco, in 2007 in Edison, New Jersey, in 2009 in Los Angeles, in 2011 in Houston, in 2013 in Detroit, in 2015 in Atlanta, in 2017 in Edison, New Jersey, and in 2019 in Los Angeles, California.

Young Jains of America

The concept of Young Jains of America (YJA) as an essential JAINA activity was born in 1989 when JAINA President Sulekh Jain asked Urmila Talsania of Chicago to lead the effort to create a youth wing for the 14–29 age group.

She initiated contact with various Jain centers and established contacts with youth coordinators. Many of these initial youth coordinators met in 1990 when the Jain Center of Greater St. Louis organized a youth camp. Bruce Costain (aka Balabhadra) was invited as the keynote speaker at that gathering. At the 1991 JAINA convention in San Francisco, YJA was born. YJA mission statement is "to be recognized nationally and internationally as an umbrella Jain youth organization for establishing a network for and among youth to share Jain heritage and religion."[20] YJA is a vehicle that the Jain youth have used to learn more about Jainism from like-minded individuals and colleagues. A by-product of that has been the opportunity to meet and interact with other youth from around North America. It evolved from the local Jain meeting at someone's house to the national conventions. YJA was more of a youth-led movement to explore the boundaries of their religion. It gave the youth a forum to discover and investigate Jainism without any intervention from the elder Jain community. Between 1989 and 1993, various youth and adult leaders came together to form what we now know as YJA. It was at that crucial meeting at the JAINA convention in Pittsburgh in 1993 that leaders came forward and committed themselves to making this entity a reality. Early on, Talsania had concluded that the youth activity could best be organized by creating six regions in North America. Regional activities could result in a national convention in the even years as the adult conventions were held every odd year. This way, every summer there is an event for the Jain youth either at the JAINA Convention or at the YJA convention. At the 1993 Convention in Pittsburgh, Talsania's proposal to have the first YJA convention in Chicago was approved. Prem Gada and Jayshree Ranka joined hands, and the first YJA convention materialized with 400 youth. Later JAINA too reorganized itself into this system of six regions. JAINA also adopted YJA's organized process of inviting bids to host conventions in a given area.

The youth who grew out of YJA created the Young Jain Professionals (YJP) in 1997 that serves youth between the ages of 24 and 39. Many of their members migrated from YJA, so there is a natural overlap between YJA and YJP. Individuals can decide whether to be members of both groups or choose a single membership. Both groups work with one another and with JAINA. The idea behind this organization has been to provide a forum for learning about and discussing issues that Jain youth face in the professional world and continue to face in their daily lives. YJP organized its first convention in January 1998 and has done several others since then. The convention topics typically include Jainism and certain professions with "violence," socially responsible investing, Jain bioethics, balancing career and family, nonviolent communication, and applying Jainism in daily life.

The World Community Service of JAINA

The World Community Service (WCS) was established in 1991 under the chairmanship of Dhiraj Shah. This JAINA committee has carried out relief operations around the world by donating more than $350,000. WCS has helped victims of major natural disasters, run medical camps, helped war victims, adopted villages, supported schools, and rebuilt villages. Annually, WCS donates several loads of medical equipment, clothes, blankets, wheelchairs, and dental chairs. In 1996, WCS became the second Indian American organization to receive the Certificate of Registration by the US Agency for International Development (USAID). With this recognition, WCS and JAINA became eligible to receive USAID funds for aid projects in India. Later, in June of that year, the Government of India also recognized JAINA as an agency under the Indo-US Bilateral Agreement. The American Red Cross gave JAINA an Institution of the Year award in 1995.

The Education Committee of JAINA

In 1989, JAINA established the Education Committee under the chairmanship of Prem Gada. Two scholars from India were sponsored for six months, and they prepared the initial research for Pathshala education material in 1991. The JAINA Education Committee established the JAINA library in Lubbock, TX, and launched the first JAINA website. In 1995, eight colorful books were published for Level 1 and Level 2 students. In 1997, Level 3 and Level 4 books were published. In 2000, the Education Committee was split into the following four committees: the library committee, the technology and website committee, the education committee, and the publication committee. Gada arranged for a meeting of Pathshala teachers in New York in 1991 at the home of Jyotiben Gandhi. The first JAINA Pathshala Teachers Convention was held in Boston in 1998. Many centers participated in the convention, and a syllabus for each grade level was refined. They decided to meet again every four years, and, in 2002, Los Angeles held the second Pathshala Convention. Today, JAINA education materials are used not only in North America but in India, Singapore, Africa, and the UK. Materials produced by the committee are sold at highly subsidized prices. Some of the notable material provided by this committee is:

1 *Jainism Religion of Compassion and Ecology* (7,000 copies, two editions).
2 *The Essence of World Religions* (10,000 copies, two editions).
3 *The Book of Compassion* (13,000 copies).
4 Jain Education and Literature CD: (5,000 copies).

Charity and donations by JAINA

JAINA's Jivdaya committee collects funds to help animal shelters and pinjrapoles. Over the years, it has raised over $50,000 that were distributed to dozens of institutions. It has partnered with the Vegetarian Society in Bombay to help with the distribution of funds. Through the efforts of this committee, it is easy for any center to channel their Jivdaya funds to any pinjrapole of their choice, even if they do not have foreign remittance certificate from the Government of India.

In 1994, a trust fund under the leadership of Mahendra Pandya to support JAINA's core activities was established in 1994. The function of the trust is to collect funds from voluntary contributions by individuals committed to JAINA's cause. Over the years it has proven to be a lifeline for JAINA. In 1997, during the Presidency of Dhiraj Shah, a permanent solution to the perennial financial woes of JAINA was implemented. This enabled JAINA to hire a paid part-time Executive Director to attend to much of the back-office work and establish a JAINA headquarters. Funding for the Patron Program began to dwindle for some time, but a later JAINA president, Anop Vora, has revived it and once again made it a vital organ of JAINA.

Becoming Jain in America

Balabhadra Bruce Costain, whose name we encountered in a couple of events in the American Jain timeline above, is a Canadian-born and Tennessee-settled Jain who adopted Jainism, inspired by Chitrabhanu in the early 1980s. He has published a book (Costain 2003) and made online videos[21] on Applied Jainism, to teach "how to make decisions that will result in increased peacefulness, happiness and love for ourselves as well as for other living beings." Charlotte Laws is another American author and animal rights activist who practices and writes about Jainism and animal rights.[22]. Laws told me:

> I adopted Jainism around 1995 while obtaining my doctorate in Religion and Social Ethics at the University of Southern California. I was specifically drawn to the idea of nonviolence or ahimsa (the central tenet of the religion). I also agree that violence can occur through words and think. Jainism captured my heart. I had been an animal advocate and vegetarian since 1981. I try not to harm living beings to the point that I even feel it is vital to make sure my yard has water to nourish plants, insects, and animals (i.e., rabbits). I try to be a role model to others and nudge people in the direction of love and compassion for all living beings via my books, articles, interviews, and speaking engagements. I have become a vegan in recent years, although I do eat the eggs of my six happy hens who live in my backyard. I adopted them from animal shelters so they would not die. I obtained my first hen (who died a few years back) via a heartbreaking Craigslist ad that read, "Free. Would make a good dinner." In addition to Jainism's emphasis on being loving and gentle concerning all living beings, I like that Jainism does not rely upon a Creator and is non-judgmental of others. It does not lean on moral absolutes in the way that many religions do. I am a relativist and believe there are many facets of truth. This is not to say that I agree with all aspects of Jainism. For example, I am not an ascetic. I believe in "mixing it up in the world" or actively pursuing a change in ways that traditional Jains might not. During my semi-formal study of Jainism at the Jain Center of Southern California, I was told by an instructor that my "activeness" is not the

Jain way. But this is not a problem for me because I hold that religion is personal, and interpretation is subjective. A world comprised of Jains would be a happier and less violent world.

In 2012, Sanghamitra took her initiation as a Jain Sadhvi (nun) inspired by the Jain nun Acharya Chandanaji. In 2015, Nisha Kapashi, 23, a native of New York, took her initiation in India. In 2016, a 33-year-old Mexican American, Tania Maynez became Sadhvi Anubhuti when Acharya Yogeesh initiated her as the second nun at Siddhayatan, a 200-acre spiritual retreat near Dallas, Texas.[23] In 2008, Tammy Herbster, a 24-year-old Indonesian American Iraq War veteran, was initiated by Acharya Yogeesh, giving her the new name, Sadhvi Siddhali Shree. Sadhvi Siddhali serves as the spiritual director of Siddhayatan, that was also founded in 2008. This has been a remarkable revival of Acharya Yogeesh's career who was involved in some controversies in 1988 in California (Haldane 1988). On his website, I found this information[24]

Acharya Shree Yogeesh has founded multiple centers. His first center, Yogeesh Ashram International, was established in 1992 in New Delhi, India. His first US-based center, Yogeesh Ashram, was established in 1994 and is located in Riverside, California. In 2004, he developed a higher secondary school, where 250 children receive education, in Haryana, India. In 2008 he established Siddhayatan Tirth, where he currently resides, in Windom, Texas. And recently, in 2014, he founded his first Europe-based ashram, Siddhayatan Estonia, in Tallinn, Estonia, Eastern Europe. All of his centers promote the universal teachings of nonviolence, spirituality, truth, total transformation, and soul awakening.

On various social media sites, Yogeesh continues to attract hundreds of thousands of followers. Unlike traditional Jain sects where gender equality is still not practiced, Yogeesh claims to be following in the footsteps of Mahavira who, for the first time in the history of the world, initiated thousands of women into his community as nuns. In 2011, when he took some of his European followers to India, he was honored by all the major Jain sects in Agra.[25] In 2017, Siddhayatan released a documentary to end global sex trafficking. In April 2019, when I visited Siddhayatan, the new temple was ready to be inaugurated, and three hills were being prepared for the installation of three images of Hindu and Jain deities. Almost half of the visitors were Indian Americans, while the other half were Caucasians.

Jainism in America: forays into academia and other new developments[26]

As Aukland (2016) notes, there has been an upsurge in the Jain community in North America to donate to American universities to establish professorships and chairs to teach and research Jainism. In 1994, two tax-exempt charitable organizations were established, Mahavir Vision Inc. and the Jain Academic Foundation of North America (JAFNA). Initially, both organizations supported scholars to write articles and books on Jainism and sponsor seminars and conferences. In 2004, Shugan Jain and others started a program called the International School for Jain Studies (www.isjs.in). As of 2019, about 1,000 students and faculty have visited India during the breaks in the summer or winter to study Jainism under this study abroad program.

In 2009, Jains under the banner of Jain Education and Research Foundation (JERF), established the first Bhagwan Mahavir endowed Professorship in Jain Studies at Florida International University in Miami, Florida. In 2011, JAINA signed an MoU with Claremont Lincoln University in California. This program to teach Jainism continued for three years until CLU changed its mission from teaching religions to training leaders. In 2014, Jains established the graduate-level program in Jainism at Claremont School of Theology, the parent institution of CLU. In 2012, the International School for Jain Studies (ISJS) started a new program *Teaching for Peace* led by Laura Hirshfield in which K-12 teachers travel to India and work with various NGOs founded by Jains. As of 2019, Jains have established or supported the teaching of Jainism at several more American universities, including Emory University, the University of North Texas, the University of California at Irvine, the University of California at Riverside, the University of California at Davis, the University of California at Santa Barbara, Loyola Marymount University, California State University at Northbridge, and California State University at Fullerton.

As noted by Anne Vallely (2000) and others, Jains in North America have developed some characteristics that are different from their counterparts in India or elsewhere. Although most cities in North America now have vibrant temples with regular ritual ceremonies, most American Jains do not perform any rituals daily, unlike Jains in India. Asceticism, that continues to be a significant hall-mark of Jainism in India, is a much de-emphasized practice in North America, due to the continued prohibition on Jain ascetics against travel. American Jains are also considerably nonsectarian as they have accommodated all the major sects of Jainism in their various temples across America. The establishment of JAINA to represent all Jains in North America, irrespective of their religious denomination, language, and regional identity, was a significant milestone. Unfortunately, such a model has not been replicated anywhere else in the Jain world. Except for a few, all the Jain centers, societies, and associations in North America were named without any sectarian name or identity, e.g. the Jain Society of Houston, the Jain Center of Southern California, etc. The use of English language in many ceremonies and rituals rather than Indian languages further makes Jainism appealing across the boundaries of regions, nations, or Indian languages. Also compared to Jain women in India, American Jain women are more prominent in their leadership roles in Jain organizations at local and national levels. American Jains are also much more active in representing Jainism in various interfaith forums. Especially American-born Jains tend to promote and practice meditation as well as veganism and animal rights more than immigrant Jains born in India or elsewhere. Thus, as Vallely has noted, Jains in India practiced environmentalism to achieve liberation, but American Jains practice environmentalism with the much more sociocentric approach. For instance, traditionally, one of the Jain Tirthankaras Neminath rejects his life of pleasures and wealth and becomes an ascetic when he comes across brutality towards animals. However, some American Jains have reinterpreted that legend to inspire Jains to become active protectors and defenders of animal rights. Rather than renouncing the worldly life, Neminath encourages some American Jains to become activists for the animal world. As is common across other American-born Asians, a large number of Jains are also marrying interfaith and interracially,[27] as seen in regular wedding announcements in *The New York Times* Sunday Edition.

As of 2019, the Jain population in the United States and Canada stands at more than 150,000 and is growing. There are currently about 70 Jain temples in North America that are listed in Appendix 3. North American Jains represent a highly educated community with particularly strong representation in medicine, engineering, teaching, and business. A significant number of Jain youth is now studying in some of the top universities of this country. Another notable feature of American Jains is their accomplishments in the trade of diamonds and other precious stones as we see in the next section.

Jain diamantaires in North America

This section highlights the remarkable success of Jain diamond traders, i.e., diamantaires in America. Up to the 1700s, India was the primary source of diamonds in the world[28] and Jains historically considered diamond trading as a nonviolent profession, according to *Bhogopabhog Vrata*, a Jain text that lists the occupations that are allowed or prohibited according to the violence involved in them. Jains seem to have ignored the violence involved in diamond mining in Africa, as shown in the reports related to "blood diamonds."[29]

Some of the Jain diamantaires started coming to the USA in the 1960s, and more joined in later decades. Some of the Jaipur-based pioneers were families of Surana (who is now a significant player in New York) and Kothari (who is now a significant player in Thailand). Many Jains started with color stones and gems and added diamonds later to their portfolios. In the early 1970s, Jain diamantaires from Mumbai and Gujarat, e.g., the Kotharis, Parikhs, Shahs, and Mehtas, established offices in New York. In the beginning, Indians were trading in only the small "bottom of the barrel" diamonds. Over the decades, India emerged as the diamond-cutting center, especially Mumbai and the cities in Gujarat, e.g., Surat, Navsari, and Valsad (Klein 2005). The rise of India, in general, was proportional to the success of Jains in this business. Although this journey started with small diamonds, over time, they continued to gain more and more influence on medium-sized and larger diamonds also. In the early 2000s, India became a major player in all kinds of diamonds, including the diamonds certified by the Gemological Institute of America.

Before World War I, Jains in Palanpur were already active in the diamond trade. India was the primary source of diamonds until the 1700s, but in 1725, after diamonds were discovered in Brazil, global trade began to emerge.[30] Since both Brazil and Goa (in India) were Portuguese colonies, diamonds that were mined in Brazil were brought to Goa. Once they were sealed as Indian products, their values increased many times to be exported from India from the port of Calcutta (now Kolkata). In the late 1800s, Cecil Rhodes founded De Beers diamond company in South Africa soon after the first diamond was discovered there (Kothari 2009, 478). Due to the Dutch and South African trade connections, Amsterdam emerged as one of the earliest diamond centers. Indian royal families remained consumers of diamonds, and India remained an essential importer during that period. As the British started employing Indians in Rangoon (Burma), demand for pure diamonds increased there. In his paper, Kaivan Munshi (2007, 6) mentions that the modern Indian diamond industry started taking shape in the 1880s when the two Palanpuri Jain merchants, Surajmal Lallubhai and Amulakh Khubhchand Parikh, moved their businesses from Bombay (now Mumbai) to Calcutta (now Kolkata) to Rangoon (Burma). This trend continued in the next centuries, and by 1937, around 25 Jain families had migrated to Antwerp. These international connections received a setback when many Indians returned to India during World War II. Before World War I, some Jain diamantaires left Palanpur (Gujarat) and established offices in Rangoon and also in Madras (now Chennai) in Southern India. The Jain temple built in Rangoon in 1914 still serves the local needs there.[31] After World War I, India was brought into increasing contact with Europe, and the Indian diamond trade also grew there. Some pioneer Jain diamantaires started doing business in Antwerp, Belgium, in the 1920s, supplying polished diamonds in India in partnership with local Jews in Antwerp (Melwani 2003; Backman 2005). However, the Great Depression of the 1930s stopped this trade. After the Jewish persecution in Europe, the Jain diamantaires returned to India. World War II ended the diamond imports from Belgium ultimately. Burmese Indians also returned to India.

Most notable among the early pioneers was Mafatlal Mehta, aka Mafat Kaka, who started several diamond companies in Antwerp, such as Jayam, Jitendra Brothers, and Jem, that helped groom his sons and others in this business. Later, he set up several offices in Los Angeles, Hong Kong, Tel Aviv, and elsewhere. Upon meeting Mother Teresa, Mehta turned into a significant philanthropist and supported several educational, health, and other charities with his trust named after his mother Diwaliben Mohanlal Mehta (Bhatt 2005).

After India's independence in 1947, the Government of India, in its socialist zeal under the first Prime Minister Jawaharlal Nehru, banned the import of diamonds in order to conserve its Foreign Exchange reserve. However, in 1962, the Indian government started giving "replenishment" licenses for the import of rough diamonds so that they could be cut and polished in India and exported to Europe (Kothari 2009, 481). This helped the government earn foreign exchange. Once again, Jains from Palanpur went ahead and established an office at Antwerp. Indian cutters enjoyed their low-price advantage and slowly advanced their trade interests by reselling diamonds back to Euro-Americans while abiding by the Indian Forex rules by maintaining the family connections between Antwerp and India (the same family kept two offices in India and Belgium). In the 1960s, De Beers allowed about half a dozen Indian companies to be sightholders, i.e., authorized bulk purchasers of rough diamonds, and soon Palanpuri Jains established offices in Belgium, the USA, Hong Kong, Japan, and Israel. The joint family system of traditional Jains was very useful in this trade that always needs a lot of mutual trust. In 1968, the Indian government passed the Gold Control Act that made the possession of gold illegal, but diamonds remained well established as a good source of employment and foreign exchange. In Gujarat alone, approximately 10 percent of the population were employed in this industry.

In his PhD dissertation and later in his chapter, Abhijit Kothari (2009) presents his research with Palanpuri Jains and their success in the diamond industry. Munshi (2007) similarly presents his analysis of the relatively more recent success of the Kathiawadi people in this industry. Both Kothari and Munshi make the following observations. The first generation of pioneer diamantaires between the late nineteenth and early twentieth century started diversifying their business interests and gained access to quality stones. They recognized the diamond trade as an independent activity and began recruiting members of their respective communities of Palanpuri, Kathiawadi, and Marwadi Jains. The second generation, between the 1950s and the 1990s, built on the strong foundations established by the first generation and recognized the competitive advantage of low-cost polishing. This was also the period in which several family members of these Jains migrated to Antwerp and other foreign centers of the diamond industry. The reliance on family members thus continued, and such global networks further established their trade internationally. Starting from the 1990s, the third generation continued to consolidate and grow the business by setting up more offices and branches in multiple locations across the world. More professionals are also being inducted, but family members continue to occupy critical positions internationally (Kothari 2009, 485).

Lalit Kothari was born in Bikaner, Rajasthan, India. He is the sixth generation in the diamond business. Gujarati Jains have dominated this industry, but people from Rajasthan have also jumped on the bandwagon in the last few decades. His was one of the first Indian companies to open an office in Los Angeles in 1960s although a few Gujaratis had already arrived in the New York area. Initially, the reputation of India was poor in diamond cutting. As Indians adopted the new technologies and machines, they are now well respected as they offer sound quality. Indians now buy and sell from all over the world, including from Israel, Belgium (Jains and other Indians dominate even the local market) and South Africa. Lalit's father was born in

Rangoon as his grandfather was there during World War II. They returned to India soon after that. They were one of the producers of gems in Burma where there used to be a thriving market for buying and producing Burmese rubies and sapphire.

Similarly, Jitubhai Shah is a prominent diamantaire in Los Angeles, the second biggest jewelry market in the USA. Some of his family members had moved to Antwerp in the 1950s, and he came to the USA in 1969 and received his undergraduate degree in 1973 in Business Administration from California State University. He went back to India to learn the diamond trade in a relative's office near the Opera House in Mumbai. After his four months of training, he started trading the loose diamonds as one of the earliest Jain pioneers in diamonds with a lot of help from family and friends. He bought his first office in 1974 where his son helped him in his business that includes jewelry manufacturing and selling expensive watches.

Udai Jain lives in Houston, and most of his nine other brothers are in the jewelry business that his older brother started in 1966 in Agra. Udai used to teach at a community college in Kota, Alwar, and Ajmer, different towns in Rajasthan and came to the USA for higher studies in 1971. In 1973, his two brothers joined him, and in 1975, two more brothers came to the USA. He received his Master's Degree in a STEM field from UC Berkeley. The rest of his brothers are now in Los Angeles, New York, Bangkok, and Mumbai. The entire family tries to meet in Jaipur annually, although all have now separate businesses. He attributes the Jains' success to their willingness to take risks and the mutual trust among Jains that lets people borrow goods for several months on credit.

Shefali Jhaveri is a diamantaire in Houston, Texas. Her father was born in 1943, and in the 1960s, his grandfather moved to Surat (Gujarat, India) for better opportunities in jewelry manufacturing there. Her son was born in the USA, who received his education in Surat, Mumbai, and Coimbatore. She works with diamond polishers in Surat and sightholders in Mumbai, Israel, and Antwerp. Her customers are in the USA, Australia, and India. She attributes the success of the diamond industry partly to the great marketing campaigns by De Beers, e.g., "Diamonds Are Forever," and "Diamonds Are a Girl's Best Friend."

One of the pioneer diamantaires in Mumbai, Jain Rasilal and Company has emerged from an office near the Opera House, now to a large office complex in Bandra Kurla Complex in Mumbai. Some other prominent diamond communities are Marwari Jains, with Bikaner as their manufacturing center, Suranas in Jaipur, Jains in New Delhi, and Digambara Jains in Coimbatore (Tamilnadu).

In 1978, Pradeep Vaidya and his brother started the color stone business, by importing them from Jaipur. Slowly they transitioned into diamonds. He did his MS in Industrial Engineering from Lehigh University in PA, and worked as an engineer for seven years in Pennsylvania but was looking to start a business. They bought diamonds from people in New York initially and learned the trade from them. They received their first consignment of

$50,000 from New York from some fellow Jain wholesalers on loan. They paid the money back to them as they sold their goods. Gradually, with their clientele, they started going to Belgium, the biggest center then, Israel, and India and started buying directly from there. Even today, however, many Jain traders trust each other with loaning consignments to each other. They had contacts in Jaipur, as his brother's wife is from there. They started with wholesale trading of diamonds and sold to stores in Dallas.

Initially, the market was dominated by Jews (Bilefsky 2003). Smaller diamonds were cut in India while bigger ones were cut in Israel and Belgium, so they started importing smaller ones from India. But in the last ten years, the trend has changed, and Gujarati Jains have done very well. They used to buy small diamonds (bottom of the barrel) from Belgium and then they produced excellent quality diamonds in India. When De Beer realized this, it started giving the bigger diamonds directly to Indians. Now, India has become the number one country in the world in terms of volume. Gujarat is the hub for cutting and Mumbai for trading. In the 1980s, Antwerp had very small number of Indians, and they used to buy from Jews there. Now it is the opposite with Indians having large offices.

Similarly, in Mumbai, now Jews can be seen lining up to purchase diamonds from Indians. Indians are now dictating the terms. Indians also innovatively computerized the entire process with online selling in the early twenty-first century. With the Gemological certificate and pictures online, Indians in India revolutionized the process. Now, American diamantaires need to go to India much less often, compared to the multiple trips required in the previous century. Rough diamonds are still acquired from South Africa, Canada, China, and elsewhere, but after polishing, the process is now all online. Buyers from across the world are now buying them from Indians in India without the need to travel there. Merchants with small offices in the previous century have now huge offices in Bandra Kurla Complex, Mumbai. In Mumbai, Venus jewels were one of the pioneers (Gujarati Jains) who digitized the process.

Initially, only Jews were given the better diamonds and Indians were given only the bottom of the barrel by De Beers, who had the monopoly on diamond mines. Every month they make up, e.g., $100 million boxes of raw diamonds, on which bidding is done. At the beginning of the twenty-first century, Indians (most of them Jains) are now the majority of sightholders who sell directly to wholesalers. Some 90 percent of all the diamonds in the world now are cut in India. In terms of dollar value, Indians have at least one-third of the global business. The Indian government kept diamond trading tax-free in the 1980s. In 1966, this export from India was about $2.8 million (Kothari 2009, 481); in 2018, it reached more than $25 billion. Now the Indian government has canceled that tax relief since there is no longer any such need.

Jain values in contemporary America

In this chapter, we encountered the chronological details of Jains in America, saw glimpses of Jain diamantaires, and other Jain initiatives in America. In addition to decorating America with new Jain temples and organizations, Jains have also enriched it by bringing precious stones, such as diamonds. Nonviolence can perhaps be called the greatest gift that the Jain tradition has shared with America and the rest of the world. This is the virtue that Mahatma Gandhi learned from a Jain mystic, Shrimad Rajchandra, that remained the central pillar in his movement against the British in South Africa and India. Nonviolence also remained the highlight of Dr. Martin Luther King's campaign for the Civil Rights in the United States. However, Jainism's nonviolence is even more relevant when about 100 people are killed due to gun violence every day in America.[32] As one of my former students tweeted, "America is in bad need of the teaching of ahimsa, but every day we slide farther away from it."[33] In addition to *ahimsa*, nonviolence, Jainism's two other precious jewels are yet to catch fuller attention of Americans, and these are *aparigraha* (nonaccumulation of worldly possessions) and *anekantavada* (doctrine of many perspectives).

The simple life inspired by *ahimsa* and *aparigraha* can substantially bring down the carbon footprint of America. Guha (2006, 149) hints in his appropriately entitled book *How Much Should a Person Consume?*, the need for both *ahimsa* and *aparigraha* by Americans:

> It is the allegedly civilized, who have decimated forests and the wildlife that previously sustained both tiger and tribal. With rifles and quest for trophies, [they] first hunted wild species to extinction; now [they] disguise [themselves] as conservationists and complain that Adivasis are getting in the way. The real "population problem" is in America, where the birth of one child has the same impact on the global environment as the birth of about seventy Indonesian children. Worse, the birth of an American dog or cat was the ecological equivalent of the birth of a dozen Bangladeshi children.

This matches with the observation by the Worldwatch Institute:[34]

> The 12% of the world's population that lives in North America and Western Europe accounts for 60% of private consumption spending, while the one-third living in South Asia and sub-Saharan Africa accounts for only 3.2%. The United States, with less than 5% of the global population, uses about a quarter of the world's fossil fuel resources—burning up nearly 25% of the coal, 26% of the oil, and 27 % of the world's natural gas. As of 2003, the U.S. had more private cars than licensed drivers, and gas-guzzling sport utility vehicles were among the best-selling vehicles. New houses in the U.S. were 38% bigger in 2002 than in 1975, despite having fewer people per household on average. Even if the average American eats 20% less meat in 2050 than in 2000, total U.S. meat consumption will be 5 million tons greater in 2050 due to population growth.

Jainism emphasizes minimizing the consumption of natural resources with its millennia-old practices such as vegetarianism and asceticism that can help manage our planetary resources. Hopefully, America will lead the world in transforming its lifestyle based on these principles. Currently, movements such as minimalism, veganism, and zero waste continue to flourish. With more than 20 million minimizing their worldly possessions,[35] 5 percent of Americans becoming vegetarians,[36] dozens of cities committing to zero waste,[37] hundreds of thousands of people following initiatives such as the Zero Waste Collective,[38] and several states and towns restricting the usage of single-use plastics,[39] these are all promising examples of *aparigraha* in action.

The third principal Jain value, *anekantavada*, is about trying to understand multiple perspectives. Although the American government is criticized for unilaterally enforcing its ideologies on countries, American people are increasingly becoming open to different views and practices as noted by some observers.[40] An increasing number of people in America are now without any religious affiliation[41] even as they continue to adopt "New Age" practices, such as yoga and meditation.[42] These open intellectual and spiritual boundaries can be seen as *anekantavada* in action and can be hope for more harmonious and peaceful societies.

The three historical surveys of Indian doctors and Ayurveda practitioners, Indian classical musicians, and Indian Jains have demonstrated how different groups of people arrived and adopted their new country in different ways. We now switch to the American K-12 school system. In Chapter 6, a case study of a Dallas suburb school system with a large number of Asian Indian students, provides us yet another glimpse of Indian Americans.

Notes

1 See www.bloomberg.com/research/stocks/people/person.asp?personId=42368468&p rivcapId=255251 (accessed May 12, 2019).
2 See www.ft.com/topics/people/Anshu_Jain (accessed May 18, 2019).
3 See http://pluralism.org/timeline/jainism-in-america/ (accessed May 13, 2019).
4 See http://content.time.com/time/covers/0,16641,19310105,00.html (accessed May 18, 2019).
5 See http://content.time.com/time/magazine/article/0,9171,993024,00.html (accessed May 18, 2019). Another article it published in that issue was "The Children of Gandhi" noting Gandhi's influence on the Dalai Lama, Martin Luther King Jr., Rosa Parks, Lech Walesa, Cesar Chavez, and others.
6 See www.thehindu.com/features/magazine/i-have-a-dream/article5048166.ece (accessed May 13, 2019).
7 See www.pbs.org/thisfarbyfaith/witnesses/james_lawson.html (accessed May 13, 2019).
8 See www-tc.pbs.org/thisfarbyfaith/transcript/episode_4.pdf (accessed May 13, 2019).
9 See www.saada.org/item/20130722-3032 (accessed May 13, 2019).
10 Dhiraj Shah received a notice with 1-A status (immediate call to serve in the military) but he contested this order and requested 1-O status (Conscientious Objector). Upon submitting books by Gurudev Chitrabhanu, on Jain philosophy, the judge excused him and all future Jains from serving in the military.
11 Jain monastic rules traditionally limit the Jain monks and nuns from traveling in any vehicle so they could never take a flight, train, bus, or car to travel either within India or outside India.

12 See www.arhumyoga.com/PatBruno.html (accessed May 12, 2019).

13 Brianne Donaldson states that there are approximately 4,000 students and 400 teachers at the Jain Sunday Schools in North America. See https://transnationala sia.rice.edu/journal/Volume-2/Issue-1/Number-2 (accessed May 15, 2019).

14 Another Jain Temple in New Jersey faced some protest from its neighbors in 1997, a phenomenon seen across the country. Most such cases end up in lawsuits with the verdict in favor of the Hindu or Jain temples. See www.nytimes.com/1997/07/14/nyregion/jain-center-opposed.html (accessed May 18, 2019).

15 See https://cdn.ymaws.com/www.jaina.org/resource/resmgr/jaina_organization/jaina_constitution_1-15-09.pdf (accessed May 13, 2019).

16 See www.jaina.org/page/pathshalabooks (accessed May 13, 2019).

17 "In 1980, the late Acharya Tulsi, along with his then-*Yuvacharya* (appointed successor), Mahaprajna, established a second ordination level, samani diksha. This level was established for two main purposes. Due to the overwhelming number of Jains living abroad, it was created to provide spiritual care and support for them. Secondly, as a result of increased interest in religious and spiritual ideas, Terapanthi Jains wanted a class of ordained scholar-educators who could participate in the various religious and academic conferences being held worldwide. As fully ordained Jain renunciants are prohibited from using transportation other than their own two feet, participation in global religious conferences was not possible. Acharya Tulsi wanted to rectify this dilemma; hence, the creation of the saman and samani order. Today there are seventy-five samanis and just one saman" (Komal Kumar 2016, 16).

18 Usually, American public schools do not teach any religion but many private schools that are run by laymen usually teach about Christianity.

19 See http://sunsite.unc.edu./jainism/ (accessed May 13, 2019).

20 See https://yja.org/mission (accessed May 13, 2019).

21 See www.youtube.com/user/appliedjainism (accessed May 12, 2019).

22 See http://charlottelaws.com/?page_id=153 (accessed May 12, 2019).

23 See www.ketr.org/post/unlikely-place-enlightened-hindu-master (accessed May 10, 2019).

24 See https://siddhayatan.org/about/ (accessed May 10, 2019).

25 See https://www.jaina.org/news/59719/Jains-Unite-and-Make-History.htm (accessed May 10, 2019).

26 See www.scpr.org/news/2013/08/18/38761/us-born-jains-make-ascetic-faith-fit-modern-life/ (accessed May 12, 2019).

27 See www.pewresearch.org/fact-tank/2017/06/12/key-facts-about-race-and-marriage-50-years-after-loving-v-virginia/ (accessed May 13, 2019).

28 See www.cbsnews.com/news/diamonds-a-history/ (accessed May 10, 2019).

29 See http://time.com/blood-diamonds/ (accessed May 10, 2019).

30 See www.cbsnews.com/news/diamonds-a-history/ (accessed May 10, 2019).

31 See www.yangongui.de/jain-temple/ (accessed May 10, 2019).

32 See https://everytownresearch.org/gun-violence-america/ (accessed May 12, 2019).

33 See https://twitter.com/glennart55/status/1122994329663016960 (accessed May 12, 2019).

34 See www.worldwatch.org/node/810 (accessed May 12, 2019).

35 See www.theminimalists.com/about/#the_mins (accessed May 10, 2019).

36 See www.forbes.com/sites/niallmccarthy/2018/08/06/who-are-americas-vegans-and-vegetarians-infographic/#4fdb57fe211c (accessed May 10, 2019).

37 See www.nationalgeographic.com/travel/lists/zero-waste-eliminate-sustainable-travel-destination-plastic/ (accessed May 10, 2019).

38 See www.instagram.com/zero.waste.collective (accessed May 10, 2019).

39 See www.businessinsider.com/plastic-bans-around-the-world-2019-4 (accessed May 10, 2019).

40 See www.newsweek.com/us-views-god-and-life-are-turning-hindu-79073 (accessed May 10, 2019).

41 See www.scientificamerican.com/article/the-number-of-americans-with-no-religious-affiliation-is-rising/ (accessed May 10, 2019).

42 See www.upi.com/Health_News/2018/11/08/Number-of-Americans-practicing-yoga-meditation-surged-in-last-six-years/4871541738659/ (accessed May 10, 2019).

6 Indian Americans and civic engagements

Although professors of Indian origin now head some of the top business schools and other universities, Indian Americans have barely started participating in the management and leadership of the K-12 school systems in America. The ability of immigrant communities to participate meaningfully in the socio-political process of their host country is dependent on the immigration and citizenship laws of that country, cohesiveness within the immigrant community, and the support of the native citizens of the host country (Mishra, 2017). As of 2019, the Indian immigrants are the second largest immigrant group in the US after their Mexican counterparts.[1] However, Indian Americans, being some of the most recent citizens of the USA, continue to be perceived as "forever foreigners" in America by the majority of the population, a significant hurdle against acceptance and participation of Indian Americans in getting elected for government bodies. Additionally, since a considerable section of the Indians in America have not been granted US citizenship due to a massive backlog in the immigration system (Cockrell, 2017), they are denied voting rights even in the local elections for their city council and school board.

In their study, Hunter and Franz (2006) present a life course model of immigrant communities with four phases, with some overlaps in these phases. In the first introductory phase, most immigrants are inward-looking with minimal public statements to disrupt the mainstream discourse. In the second recognition phase, immigrant groups gather enough socio-economic and financial resources to make their presence felt by the American state and the American public. In the third negotiation phase, these groups negotiate their identities vis-à-vis the American culture. Finally, in the fourth stage of establishment, the groups gain enough wider American public and state recognition to make them accepted as a "normal" American grouping. They go on to state that most post-1965 groups are yet to reach the final stage of establishment. They also ask the questions related to education in the public schools:

> How recent immigrant religions will engage these challenges remains unclear. Will they create after-school and weekend religious education courses? Will, they set up separate schools? Will they school their children at home? At the same time, how will public schools accommodate

the presence of more and more children from the Hindu, Sikh, Buddhist, and Muslim communities?

Such are the questions that Khyati Joshi (2006) also tackles in her monograph. She provides some interesting insights into Indian Americans and their next generations who are born in the United States. Being non-White and non-Christian, although they are "unmeltable" double minorities from both racial and religious perspectives, their relatively higher economic and educational achievements help them survive and continue to enjoy their American dream. Joshi presents two versions of the second-generation Indian Americans. Most of the Indian Americans who were born in the USA in the 1960s, the 1970s, and the 1980s were perhaps the only Asian American student in their respective classrooms. Their classmates had probably never heard of India. Their connections to Indian culture were tenuous at best with little possibility of Bollywood films or temples in their immediate surroundings. In contrast, kids born in the 1990s onwards had at least a few more Asian or even Indian Americans in their classrooms who perhaps might wear some Indian cultural marks, such as bindi or a tattoo. This generation grew up loving Bollywood (and Hollywood) films and attending their Sunday school classes for Indian culture at their neighborhood Hindu or Jain temples.

Despite a more Indian culturally based upbringing at home, however, both groups continue to have a similar experience outside of their home. For instance, as Joshi describes in her 2013 chapter, in Metro Atlanta, Christianity is "constructed as the normal against which 'other' is compared to the other's advantage." According to her, Christian normativity, which is, at times, subtle, permits, and maintains patterns of oppression "by neglect, omission, erasure, and distortion." She points out that Christianity dominates all the seasonal celebrations and decorations such as the "Easter Bunny, Santa Claus, Christmas trees, garlands, wreaths," etc. This Christian domination in America often goes unnoticed, and anyone noticing or challenging this is rejected as abnormal. Indian Americans, most of them non-Christians, are also neither black nor white, and being a "double minority," they remain largely invisible on the Southern racial map since, as Joshi goes on to say, "concepts of race remain largely defined by the dyadic paradigm of Black and White."

Joshi and Adams (2007) mention several examples of this Christian dominance as the US national culture in American K-12 school system. For instance, Christmas is the only religious festival that enjoys the national holiday, Christian prayers are said at school athletic events and other assemblies, such as city council and school district's board of trustees' meetings. Just as Joshi observed in Metro Atlanta, I found several similar examples in Dallas Metroplex in Texas. For instance, Good Friday is another major Christian holiday that enjoys a school holiday in Texas, although it is designated as a "weather day." In her 2013 article, Joshi focused on one particular incidence of the portrayal of Hindu god Ganesh that galvanized Hindus in Atlanta. In this chapter, I share some of my participant observations as I became involved in Coppell School District's 2016 election process to elect its board of trustees. I was also involved in the petition to ask for Diwali as a school holiday.

As in many Asian countries, people in India continue to harbor the American dream (Dhingra 2012). As mentioned earlier, unlike the previous laws that restricted immigration from Asia, the Immigration and Nationality Act of 1965 started changing the demographic makeup of the American population and gave more opportunities to Asians (Halter et al. 2014). In the early 1970s, when Indians started coming to America, they were mostly the "skilled workers," such as scholars, engineers, and doctors (Helweg and Helweg 1990). In the 1980s and the 1990s, more business-driven immigrants and other professionals started pouring into the "land of opportunity." By the 1990s, with the rising demand in information technology, there was an influx of computer software professionals. Today, the American IT industry appears to be dominated by Indian Americans, especially because some of them are now leading the major companies such as Microsoft, Adobe, and Google. Indians have made breakthroughs in several different fields, pushed boundaries, held positions of power, and contributed to the economic as well as intellectual growth of the country. As of 2019, America is home to approximately five million Indian Americans. In many contexts, they are referred to as the "model minority," as they are one of the highest qualified ethnic groups with one of the highest median household income.[2] As of 2019, Indian Americans have already emerged on the American political scene nationwide. There are 5 lawmakers in the US Congress (1 in the US Senate and 4 in the US House of Representatives), 13 state legislators, 5 state senators, 1 attorney general, 8 mayors, 3 vice mayors, 30 members in different city councils, 1 county clerk of court, 8 judges, and 19 school board trustees. All of these elected officials are listed on www.IAImpact.org (accessed January 22, 2019).

As mentioned earlier, Indian Americans compose only 1 percent of the total American population. However, in recent years, Indian students are now a significant demographic segment in several American school districts. Although US census laws prohibit counting by religion or national origin, the racial category of "Asian" broadly tells us the percentage of students in each school district. For instance, as of 2019, in Coppell school district, a suburb of Dallas in Texas, and Milpitas and Irvine school districts in California, almost 50 percent of students are identified as Asians. Cupertino in California, however, must be the only school district in America where nearly 74 percent of students are Asians. However, despite their large numbers, Indians in particular and Asian Americans, in general, are inadequately represented in the local government positions, such as on the school boards, city councils, or among school teachers. Studies show that there is a link between the formal and the informal methods of civic engagement of a community in a society. The informal way should lead to official civic engagement.[3] This deeper engagement will also help Indian Americans keep an eye on tax rates and keep them aware of the city's fiscal policies.

Although the City of Coppell is just over 14 square miles in area, the Coppell school district spans over 23 square miles in the cities of Coppell, Irving, Dallas, and Grapevine.[4] As of 2019, the Coppell School System remains one of the largest employers in Coppell, with over 1,200 employees. It is comprised of 18 campuses serving almost 13,000 students in grades PreK–K–12. As of 2019, the demographic data[5] indicate that Asians students comprise nearly 50 percent in Coppell ISD, but there is only 1 (out of 7 members) member of Asian Indian heritage on the school board of trustees, who was elected in 2018. Texas gives us a vantage point for research on the new emerging identity of Indian Americans as an onlooker of the process of a local election. Let us briefly look at the recent growth and demographic make-up of the schools of Coppell ISD (Independent School District).

Challenges for the Indian Americans in Coppell ISD

Within Coppell ISD's boundary, certain neighborhood areas are mostly inhabited by the Indian population. Addressing a similar situation for the Hispanic community, several Dallas area ISD residents filed lawsuits to reform their respective school board's voting process. According to these lawsuits, the "at-large" voting process was diluting the votes of minorities who wanted to elect their minority representative at least for their respective neighborhoods with a Hispanic majority. By holding at-large elections and requiring a district-wide majority vote, candidates run for specific seats but do not represent a particular geographic area. These lawsuits were filed in various school boards in Texas and California and were won by minority plaintiffs.[6]

Even though most of the Indian American parents send their kids to public schools, they lack the awareness and engagement in the local school board (and city council) elections. Asian Americans, in general, are still learning about the *modus operandi* of school boards and their election processes. Most of the immigrants do not even know that they have the right to choose their representative as a board member. Worse, there is little motivation to find out about the candidates who run for school board positions. Unlike national elections, local elections such as for school boards and city councils, tend to get less coverage in the media and this shows up in the low voter turnout for local elections compared to national ones. With this backdrop of local politics, I now present the case study of my own (unsuccessful) bid for one of the seats for the school board trustees for Coppell ISD.

Running for the Coppell School Board Election

I moved to Coppell with my family in 2010 and bought a house there in 2012. With another friend, I became involved in organizing my community, especially after a couple of incidents. First, we heard about different burglary incidents in our neighborhood. So, we decided to hold a neighborhood watch meeting with Coppell Police. Also, we were surprised by the destruction of dozens of large trees in our area. With some of my neighbors, we approached the Coppell city council and the Mayor who did not offer any help to our neighborhood. These were the couple of events that motivated me to get more involved with local government and city affairs. In February 2016, accidentally I came across an announcement on Coppell Gifted Association Facebook page, it was looking for nominations for Coppell ISD (CISD) Board of Trustees. So, I went ahead and filed for this election by faxing a couple of pages of my application form. Within an hour of submitting my application, my application form appeared on the CISD website. And soon I started receiving calls from local media and eventually from local political clubs. My first interview was published in one of the local newspapers, *Coppell Gazette.* [7] It was then that I realized that I was in the middle of a firestorm. What I initially assumed to be a small school-related volunteer process suddenly appeared to be an intensely watched political process from all directions, at all levels. From February to the final Election Day in May 2016, it took almost every waking minute of my life.

On the one hand, it is a privilege to live in a country that gives democratic rights to its citizens even at this grassroots level, where citizens decide whom they would like to trust with their tax money. Hence the name Board of Trustees. At the same time, as I began my campaign, I quickly realized that less than 10 percent of the voters use their democratic right. From the very first step, the whole process was one of the most enriching and learning experiences for me. Early on in the process, I also learned that I could get the voters list from past elections from the Dallas county election office.

One of my earliest lessons in pursuing local politics was to design a message that would appeal to broad sections of the society. As an immigrant from India and as a professor of Hinduism, most of my articles and presentations and courses so far have been limited to people interested in India or Indian Americans. But this election process reminded me that I am an American citizen, in addition to being a scholar of Indian religions and Environmental Ethics. So, one of my friends advised me to highlight my role as a teacher who receives students from different high schools across Texas and beyond. While some of my Indian friends were excited to see an Indian running for this election, the challenge was to get the support from non-Indians to a person with different skin color, race, religion, and accent. So, the message of an educator, passionate for education, became my first slogan.

The entire process of election campaign became a process for me to reach out to several new community centers. On Sunday, March 27, 2016, I visited the newly inaugurated Hindu temple called Radha Govind Dham, in Valley Ranch, Irving. It was their first celebration of the Holi festival in which an entire parking lot was cordoned off and people (of mostly Hindu origin but also some Caucasians) threw colors at each other and enjoyed Hindu picnic snacks that were being sold at different stalls. This Hindu temple is an affiliate center of Radha Madhav Dham in Austin and was inaugurated on January 24, 2016. The devotees here welcomed me as a professor of Hinduism running for the school board election. In the evening, I visited the home of an elderly Indian couple for their weekly Vipassana meditation session based on Theravada Buddhism. Here, the devotees welcomed me as a professor teaching Buddhism and other religions, running for an election of the school board.

On March 29, 2016, a friend hosted the first public meeting for this election that was attended by about a dozen neighbors from various areas of Coppell and Irving. In the meeting, it was noted that each one of us has to become the center of our circles, i.e., each one of us has to take responsibility to make sure that all our neighbors and friends go out and vote. The word was now spreading that for the first time in the history of Coppell ISD, a professor and an Indian American was running to join their board of trustees. And my dual identity was still being debated among my friends. Should I run as a professor or as an Indian American? The consensus soon emerged in favor of former and helped me in reaching broadly to all the citizens within the Coppell ISD boundary. Some voters did not vote for me after asking me outside the voting location if I was a Christian.[8]

On March 31, 2016, the *Dallas Morning News* published the voter guide with my (and other candidates') views on different aspects of Coppell ISD and its schools.[9] During the entire election process, my Indian friends kept asking me basic questions about voter registration, voting locations, etc. It was just too much for us to learn as we were recent immigrants. Other issues that were discussed often were extracurricular activities such as the Science Fair and the Math Olympiad. Most of my friends agreed that Coppell ISD should support such extra-curricular activities. I also discovered that despite having a significant population of students of Indian heritage, no Indian language was being offered at Coppell High School although Spanish, Chinese, Japanese, German, French, and Latin were being offered there. One of my friends shared the example of our neighboring school district, Hurst-Euless-Bedford ISD, that has introduced Hindi as an optional language. However, the dilemma to maintain the Indian identity or to become part of the proverbial "melting pot" continued throughout the election process and beyond. The need for an Indian language was quickly challenged by one of my other Indian friends who mentioned,

Instead of focusing on Indianizing the education, the focus should be on how to make the funds available for a better quality of teachers and quality of education. Instead of digitizing the books and building sports arenas, get more paper books. CISD's reputation is not because of the great teaching but because of "effective" Asian parenting. This situation needs to change. This campaign should not be "for Indians, by Indian, of Indians." We need to think about the greater good and involve others too. The results we see so far are more from parenting and demographics than the school itself. Thus, the focus should be improving the quality of teaching, teacher to student ratios, and overall education. Let's not make it us Indians vs. rest. There will be different avenues to promote culture and awareness. No one is against adding Indian language to school. But to me, there are more critical issues with the school where we pay high taxes and don't see the quality compared to other ISDs.

To which another Indian friend responded:

As an Indian American that came to the United States in 1973 and studied entirely in the US system from kindergarten onwards, I see a tremendous need for us to have representation. As a high school student, I was one of only two Indians in a high school class of 419 kids. It was difficult many times to explain your identity to your peers. All other major communities are represented in these settings. Why, for example, should our children learn Chinese, Arabic, or French in the school system? Why not Sanskrit and Hindi?

And finally, the consensus emerged around this sentiment:

The first thing we should do is show our active participation in society and give something back to this country (other than just taxes and doing something for Indians). Once we show our presence and participation, it will be easy to get to our language(s) and other things. Let's vote for A and become more active in society, we need our participation first in the process, PTOs, and boards. The minimum we can do is to register to vote and go vote without any excuses.

Even with all such efforts, however, I did not win the 2016 CISD election. The first Asian Indian to win the CISD election was Manish Sethi in 2018. In 2017, Vatsa Ramanathan became the first Indian American to join a school board in North Texas and in 2019, Gopal Ponangi was elected for the Frisco School Board, also in the Dallas Metroplex. According to Vatsa:

After moving to Allen, I was looking to start a business. Coming from a family of educators (my father has built two schools in Mysore, India), I thought of the education field. I started looking for places to build a school. I also tried to get a franchise for the education network. In 2008, I got a call from a realtor about a school on sale. So, I liked and bought this school. I started getting involved in the chamber of commerce. They had a workshop called Leadership Allen, and I enrolled in that. I started building my network with other entrepreneurs. I learned about Allen City and other officials of the city, including the Mayor, the councilmen, and the presidents of different committees, etc. I shared the story of my family being in the education field. One school board member suggested that I should try to join the Allen ISD team for strategic planning. I applied and was selected in that team. It was a great experience working for eight months. We came up with a mission and vision statement for the Allen

ISD that serves as a strong foundation for various Allen ISD programs that we have currently, such as vocational training and dual credit. We came up with a $300 million bond, and fortunately, Allen ISD voters approved this bond. With my growing network, I became the vice president of Allen Parks, joined the Allen library board. I funded the robotics program entirely by donating to their endowment fund. I also joined the Rotary Club board. With my intensive involvement in several Allen organizations, I gained the confidence of the people. I ran for the school board in 2013 but lost the election. After I lost the election, I emailed [the elected one] stating that from now on, I am not your opponent but am your supporter. She forwarded this note to a local newspaper. People appreciated my positive support for the school system. I continued working on several teams and boards for the Allen City and Allen ISD. It was never about any personal gain but to be able to contribute to the community in all ways possible. After a school board member suddenly resigned, I applied for this position. Fortunately, out of 40 applicants, I was selected. After I joined the board, in the next election cycle, I ran again and won the election this time. Even as an incumbent, I worked very hard on the campaign and got about 70% of the votes.

Despite my election loss, in 2017, while researching the Indian diaspora for this monograph, I discovered that Diwali is celebrated in grand style in the Caribbean countries where Indians have continued many of their traditions, even after a century since their first arrival there. In contrast, in America, although Indian parents tell stories to connect their kids with Indian culture (Narayan 2002), in many cases, they fail to give a convincing explanation for many of their religious rituals and myths, as Joshi explains (2006, pp. 15–33). In the same vein, Mody (2013) argues, based on her research with Indian American students in New Jersey, that religion remains an essential phenomenon for minority students as their identity is formed in early school years. However, most American public schools continue to ignore this vital aspect of their increasingly diverse student demographics. For instance, although almost two dozen school systems in New York, New Jersey, Pennsylvania, and Maryland have added Asian holidays, such as Diwali, Ramadan, and the Chinese New Year to their school calendars, none of the school systems elsewhere in the country have taken this critical step to reflect their diverse student population.[10] In Appendix 6, I share my conversation with the manager of DesiPlaza, a local TV channel in the Dallas area, Texas. As Long (2020) notes, most Indians are not comfortable raising the issue of cultural or racial differences, and this tension is reflected in this conversation as well.

Towards a more inclusive K-12 school system

There are several ways, K-12 school systems can be more inclusive and pluralistic.

1   On Good Friday and Easter Monday, several school districts are closed for professional development day. Similarly, on Diwali, Lunar Year, and Ramadan, they should have a professional development day (no classes). Almost 20 school districts have done this elsewhere in New Jersey, New York, Maryland, and Pennsylvania but the southern states have yet to follow suit.

2   Prominent books by Asian American authors[11] should be considered for K-12 Language Arts classes. Many of these authors have been winners of significant prizes such as the Booker or Pulitzer, some of these titles have been adapted for Hollywood films as well.

3   K-12 students currently have the option of learning other European languages, such as Spanish as a foreign language. Although several universities and colleges across North America offer Asian language classes, in the Dallas Metroplex, only Hurst-Euless-Bedford School District offers Asian language classes.[12] We should do this for other school districts as well, especially, where there is a sizeable student population of Asian heritage.

4   History and geography textbooks for middle and high schools should be carefully reviewed and revised as some of the information presented in them has several stereotypes and biases that our teachers should be made aware of.

5   Many high schools have Muslim or Chinese student clubs to foster solidarity and awareness of their own heritage, Indian heritage students should also be inspired by such initiatives to promote leadership skills.

6   Other school districts should also support the teaching of yoga and meditation as the Dallas school district is doing. The latest scientific research has shown the many physical and mental health benefits of such training.

7   Some school districts celebrate Peace Day in the Fall. Similarly, Mahatma Gandhi's birthday on October 2 should be marked as nonviolence day.[13] Portraits of Dr. King and Mahatma Gandhi should be displayed in all schools to promote racial and cultural equality and inclusion.

8   Schools should invite local Asian American (and other) professors and authors to their classes to diversity their author-visits.

9   School music lessons should include Indian and Chinese musical pieces.

10 For their field trips, students can be taken to nearby Asian cultural centers.

11 With the separation of church and state, we cannot teach *of* any religion, but we should teach *about* major world religions, especially, the traditions from China and India where religion and culture are almost synonymous. When we keep "religion" out of our school, we are also keeping our students ignorant of Asian cultures, effectively throwing the baby out with the bathwater.

12 As Ali Michael (2015) notes, citing a 2014 report by the National Center for Education Statistics, over 85 percent of the K-12 American teachers are White. However, only 52 percent of the public school students were White and almost half of the students were non-Whites (16 percent Black, 24 percent Hispanics, 5 percent Asians, and 1 percent American Indians),

according to 2011 data. Notably, in urban areas, the majority of students are non-Whites, but the majority of teachers are Whites. Our school administrators need to proactively hire more non-White teachers and educate the existing teachers and staff on race and other diversity issues.

Notes

1 See www.asamnews.com/2016/06/15/Hindu-americans-are-now-the-second-larges
   t-immigrant-group-in-the-u-s-and-the-richest/ (accessed May 12, 2019).
2 "RAD Diaspora Profile: The Indian Diaspora in the United States." (Washington,
   DC: Migration Policy Institute, 2014). Available at: www.migrationpolicy.org/sites/
   default/files/publications/RAD-IndiaII-FINAL.pdf (accessed May 13, 2019).
3 "Civic engagements does not focus on the more formal participation in such political processes as voting and campaigning for political positions but examines informal civic engagement that occurs through houses of worship, ethnic organizations, festivals and banquets, and other non-governmental agencies. And certainly, there is a link between the formal and the informal – the informal civic engagement leads to formal civic engagement" (Brettell and Danahay, 2011), pp. 167–193.
   Through various organizations the immigrants gradually spread their network and encourage business, culture and education and try to participate in American society. Through the informal civic engagements immigrants develop links to and even enter into broader, more formal, civic engagements,
4 See www.coppellisd.com/page/385 (accessed May 13, 2019).
5 See www.coppellisd.com/Page/12649 (accessed May 13, 2019).
6 See http://mobile.edweek.org/c.jsp?cid=25919821&bcid=25919821&rssid=25919811&
   item=http%3A%2F%2Fapi.edweek.org%2Fv1%2Few%2F%3Fuuid%3D08EBC4A6-
   7D2B-11E2-8124-098101ADD654 (accessed May 13, 2019).
7 See http://starlocalmedia.com/coppellgazette/unt-professor-vies-for-seat-on-coppell-isd-
   board/article_ff3fc172-df34-11e5-91d3-bb8b9c70dcba.html (accessed May 13, 2019).
8 As Suhag Shukla (2018) notes, "Ami Bera (D-CA), an Indian American born in California, who was only the second from the community after Dalip Singh Saund to be elected to the U.S. Congress, was targeted by Sikh separatists over the semantics used to describe the horrific anti-Sikh riots in the wake of Prime Minister Indira Gandhi's assassination by her Sikh bodyguards nearly 35 years ago in New Delhi. He used the term 'riots' and not 'genocide' or 'pogrom.' Ro Khanna (D-CA) faced dark insinuations of loyalty to India in a previously failed quest for a congressional seat, before he ultimately triumphed. Tulsi Gabbard (D-HI), the first Hindu elected to the U.S. Congress, who has no Indian ancestry, nevertheless is pelted by racist and anti-Hindu bigotry during every election cycle. Just last month, before Gabbard handily won a primary challenge, she was targeted by an internet portal, infamous for its voluminous efforts to force American cities to take down statues celebrating Mahatma Gandhi's non-violence movement, for having met with Modi. This, even though the Indian prime minister was embraced by both Presidents Barack Obama and Donald Trump, personally has met with dozens of U.S. Congressional leaders on multiple occasions, and has even addressed a joint session." Available at: https://thediplomat.com/2018/09/american-hindu
   s-or-hindutva/ (accessed May 13, 2019).
9 See http://c3.thevoterguide.org/v/dallasmuni16/candidate-detail.do?id=14590239 (accessed May 10, 2018).
10 See www.change.org/p/coppell-school-board-of-trustees-and-superintendent-designa
   te-diwali-a-professional-development-day-for-coppell-school-district-no-classes (accessed May 13, 2019).

11 See www.huffpost.com/entry/south-asian-writers_b_5585850 (accessed May 13, 2019).

12 See www.dallasnews.com/news/education/2012/12/20/hurst-euless-bedford-isd-offers-asian-language-option-not-readily-found-hindi (accessed May 10, 2019).

13 See www.un.org/pga/72/2017/10/02/international-day-of-non-violence/ (accessed May 10, 2018).

7 Conclusion

Before America, there were "Indians," i.e., indigenous or native communities, now known as American Indians or Native Americans. As noted by Corrigan and Winthrop (2018), by the twenty-first century, it has once again become a land of minorities where people from almost every country have now come and settled. Also, according to Jones (2019), America is no longer a White Christian majority nation because only 41 percent now belong to that category. As of 2019, almost two-thirds of the 58 million Hispanics are of Mexican origin, most of whom identify themselves as "Indians," i.e., American Indians[1] (ibid.). The Asian Indians that we met in this book and the American Indians, both "Indians," stand at almost five million each. These minorities drawn from across the world, especially after the 1965 immigration reform, continue to make America a land of pluralism as well, where every religion manifests in all kinds of festivals, colors, customs, tastes, and traditions. This diversity continues to be most prominent in states such as California that developed a distinct progressive identity since the 1900s when Indians (and other Asians) started settling there. In the twenty-first century, Indians continue to make their presence felt in states such as New York, New Jersey, Texas, Arizona, and many more. In a video made by Prager University with more than a million views, Larry Schweikart asserts that the United States "invented" modern religious tolerance.[2] Corrigan and Winthrop (2018) similarly state that among the Western nations, the USA was the first to define the state separate from religion. They also say that American religious history can also take credit for ending slavery, for philanthropic efforts to help the poor, for social reform, for women's movements, for peace movements, and social justice. In the same vein, they acknowledge that minorities have been discriminated or persecuted since the beginning of America, starting with Native Americans, to Jews, to Catholics, to Pentecostals, to African Americans, to Japanese Buddhists, to Muslims, to Hindus and Sikhs from India.

For instance, Valarie Kaur, in her documentary, *Divided We Fall* (Kaur et al. 2008), travels to 14 American cities to examine the hate crimes against the Sikhs in the aftermath of September 11, 2001. She records that her grandfather Kehar Singh arrived in the USA in 1913 and worked as a farmer for decades. She and her brother, both third-generation Americans must continue to clarify, especially at sensitive moments. such as after 9/11, that they are as

Americans as anybody else who is born here. At the beginning of the film, she painfully asks the question, what story should she tell about America? A tale of hatred or love? She interviews the brother of Balbir Singh Sodhi who was killed in Arizona, just four days after the 9/11 attacks. Less than a year later, Balbir's other brother was also killed in California. Many other Sikh men were asked to remove their turbans "to mainstream themselves" which raises the question, how can they mainstream themselves if their skin color will always remain brown even in their second or third generation? Such was also the case with the late Sunil Tripathi who committed suicide just before the Boston Marathon Bombing in 2013 but was wrongly accused on social media of being a suspect.[3]

Despite such challenges that Indian Americans continue to face across America, as Levitt (2007) notes, below the radar of most Americans and the media, Indian Americans continue to make inroads in almost every American sphere. One prominent example that begins her monograph is the Swadhyaya Parivar, a new religious movement that started in India but now has a presence in more than two dozen states of the USA as well as in Canada, Trinidad, Fiji, and Suriname (Jain 2011). What does, hopefully, appear on the American radar is the regular White House celebrations for non-Christian festivals, such as Diwali and Eid, significant festivals for Hindus and Muslims, respectively. After all, immigrants are never expected to shed their religious ties even as millions of them leave their countries of origin and adopt American citizenship, as Prothero notes (2006), citing Will Herberg from the book *Protestant, Catholic, Jew*. Religious parts of their identities remain instrumental as they settle in their new homes in America with the same goals of having a better life for their families. Many Indian immigrants also achieve their Indian or Hindu dream as they live their American dream while settling down in the USA.

The Indian diaspora, the largest diaspora in the world, as noted earlier, is also responsible for making India the first country in the world to receive remittances amounting to more than $80 billion from around the globe, according to the Migration and Development Brief by the World Bank in 2018. China, Mexico, the Philippines, and Egypt come next in the list of countries with high remittances from their respective diasporas.[4] In addition to such financial transnational connections that Indians make, new religious movements are the other principal means for their global citizenship that Levitt tries to advocate while critiquing Martha Nussbaum and Amartya Sen, who also support global citizenship, albeit of a secular variety. In this book, we saw the same religious transnational links that Jains enjoy. Two other variations of globalized connections are demonstrated by the lenses of Indian classical music and Ayurveda, not often highlighted in the discussions about globalized identities of Indian Americans. Most of the Indians did not come to the USA to seek asylum from any persecution in their home country, but they came due to some sort of social or cultural connections that they already had with America. As noted by Levitt, that connection reaches Indians either through Hollywood, the media, or even the American higher education system, especially in the engineering or medical fields. Despite this heavy influence of American culture and the education system, we find many Indians reviving or resurrecting their Indian classical music or their indigenous healthcare system such as Ayurveda as they settle in the USA. Even the K-12 education system is now waking up to the increasing demographic presence of Indian Americans, at least in some states such as California, New Jersey, New York, and Texas, as we saw in this book.

As Diana Eck (2001) mentions, the American national motto *E Pluribus Unum* cannot limit itself to one religion or one ethnicity. She notes the three models of American society. First is the exclusionary model in which the non-Whites and non-Christians are rejected. Such hatred, although muted, often resurfaces against Indian Americans and other non-Whites and non-Christians. For instance, according to the 2018 report on hate crimes released by the Federal Bureau of Investigation, attacks against Hindus continue to increase as exemplified by the killing of an Indian software engineer in Kansas City in 2017 (Dutt 2017).[5] Second is the melting pot model best exemplified by the ex-Governor of Louisiana, Bobby Jindal the first Indian American to run for American presidential election in 2015. As noted by Mishra (2017), Jindal not only converted to Catholicism but announced, "I am done with all this talk about hyphenated Americans, we are not Indian-Americans, African-Americans, Irish-Americans."[6] This melting away of one's ethnicity, race, or religion to become a "mainstream" American is increasingly challenged by the "Salad Bowl" theory or the idea of pluralism that goes beyond tolerance or acknowledgment of various religions, races, or ethnicities. Even the seemingly different traditions such as Buddhism and Judaism, or Hinduism and Christianity can be favorably compared to see interesting similarities in them. This comparison is noted by several academics, practitioners, authors, and theologians in the film *The Asian & Abrahamic Religions: A Divine Encounter in America* by Krell et al. (2011), an interesting example of people of various communities engaging, understanding, and respecting each other's traditions and cultures. This idea of pluralism comes close to *Ekam Sat Vipra Bahudha Vadanti*, i.e., the truth is one, sages call it by various names, as mentioned in the oldest Hindu text, the *Rig Veda*. The divinity is ultimately one, but everybody can and does describe it in multiple ways. Each perspective must be respected and must be allowed to flourish in its own identity. Although some observers, such as Lisa Miller,[7] have already noted the increasingly pluralistic worldview of many Americans, there are several institutional and structural roadblocks and bottlenecks to be overcome. Although diversity and inclusion have many proven advantages,[8] unfortunately, as the 2019 Pew surveys[9] show, the overwhelming majority of Americans oppose proactive inclusion of diverse races and ethnicities in hiring, correlating diversity with low employee quality and ignoring the historical racial injustices.[10]

We shall overcome, one day!

Notes

1 See www.nytimes.com/2011/07/04/nyregion/more-hispanics-in-us-calling-themselve s-indian.html (accessed May 13, 2019).
2 See www.prageru.com/videos/religious-tolerance-made-america (accessed May 13, 2019).
3 This was examined in detailed in a 2015 documentary *Help Us Find Sunil Tripathi.* Available at: www.imdb.com/title/tt4087340/ (accessed June 6, 2019).
4 See https://economictimes.indiatimes.com/nri/forex-and-remittance/india-to-retain-top -position-in-remittances-with-80-billion-world-bank/articleshow/66998062.cms (accessed May 13, 2019).
5 See www.hafsite.org/hate-crimes-against-hindus-continue-rise-fbi-stats-show (accessed May 13, 2019).
6 See www.npr.org/2015/11/18/456518086/unhyphenated-bobby-jindal-disappointed-india n-americans (accessed May 13, 2019).
7 See www.newsweek.com/us-views-god-and-life-are-turning-hindu-79073 (accessed May 13, 2019).
8 See www.forbes.com/sites/forbeshumanresourcescouncil/2019/05/03/driving-diversity-a nd-inclusion-in-the-workplace/#5d93ad0a2436 (accessed May 11, 2019).
9 See www.pewsocialtrends.org/2019/05/08/americans-see-advantages-and-challenges-in-countrys-growing-racial-and-ethnic-diversity/ (accessed May 11, 2019).
10 See https://qz.com/work/1614747/americans-like-diversity-at-work-but-only-in-theory/ (accessed May 10, 2019).

Appendix 1

The Jain Society of North Texas

Anant Jain

In the mid-1970s, there were fewer than 30 Jain families in the Dallas/Fort Worth Metroplex area. They started to perform some religious activities, such as rituals, in their homes, especially during the Jain festivals. With limited knowledge of their traditions, they researched and joined together to discover their Jain heritage. By the early 1980s, there were still fewer than 50 Jain families but with growing children. In 1982, Jain of all sects decided to establish a unified Jain society, at a meeting over dinner. The members started meeting monthly at different community centers around the Metroplex. Pathshala classes were started for children born in the 1970s. Eventually, the group organized itself as the Jain Society of North Texas (JSNT). At the first meeting, held on September 3, 1983, the members elected their first Board of Directors and adopted the constitution and bylaws. JSNT received incorporation in October 1983 and tax exemption as a 501(c)(3) from the Inland Revenue Service on February 15, 1984.

On June 30, 1988, the Society purchased a church building at 538 Apollo Road in Richardson, which became the first Jain Center in North Texas. Realizing the need to add the temple, Sunday school, and kitchen, to this facility, a building expansion program was started in 1992 to expand it from 2,100 square feet to 2,800 square feet. This was followed by an auspicious Pratishtha Mahotsav on July 11, 1993. Two Tirthankara images, Lord Parshvanath in Śvetāmbara tradition and Lord Mahavir in Digambara tradition, were installed on a common altar with a Namokar Mantra Shila in the center. Through a vibrant Pathshala program, children's education in Jainism continued to be the primary motivation of the Society. Realizing the growth in number of Pathshala children, the JSNT leadership began to realize the impending need to expand. In 1997, it acquired a 5.6-acre tract of land in the adjoining city of Garland. By 2005, there were over 300 families on the JSNT roster. The leadership started drawing up plans to build on the Garland tract. The need was not only to expand the Pathshala from two classrooms to eight classrooms, but also to allow for an enhanced, ritualistic authenticity of each Jain tradition, while retaining the unity within the diverse traditions. However, due to sudden depression affecting the US economy, the plan to build a new center in Garland had to be shelved in favor of buying, on

January 20, 2010, an existing, more cost-effective facility located in Dallas at 11321 Webb Chapel Road (formerly a BAPS Swaminarayan Temple), with a total land area of 2.38 acres.

After remodeling the Webb Chapel facility, JSNT moved there in 2011 and sold the Apollo Center in Richardson. The Webb Chapel complex is an integrated complex of three buildings. It has a two-story brick building, a single-story building with two adjoining temples under one common roof: a Śvetāmbara Temple, a Digambara Temple, and a residential building for general purposes. There is parking for 250 cars. The two-story building is called Jinendra Varniji Bhavan, named after one of the best-known Jain scholars of the twentieth century, known for his five-volume *Jainendra Siddhanta Kosha* and *Saman Suttam*, an ecumenical compilation of Jain verses accepted by all Jain sects. On the second floor of this building, there is a large kitchen, a large dining hall, six classrooms, shoe rooms, and miscellaneous equipment and storage facilities. The second floor is comprised of a large assembly hall with two stages, a library, and office, with a large, multipurpose area behind the stages, consisting of several rooms used for Samayika, green rooms, board meetings, and for other activities as required.

The Digambara temple, named Bhagwan Adinath Digambara Jain Mandir, has three images carved in the Digambara tradition and facing East: an image of Lord Adinath in the center, with a, image of Lord Mahavira on the left and an image of Lord Shantinath on the right. Lord Mahavira *pratima* was already a ritually established image at the Apollo Center in Richardson. The three images are installed on a high altar. The altar and the two new images are carved from the white Italian marble by expert sculptors from Rajasthan, India. Before they were shipped from Jaipur, the Lord Adinath and Lord Shantinath images underwent elaborate rituals *Panchakalyanak Pratishtha* in Jaipur, conducted in accordance with Jain scriptures and in conjunction with a huge *Image Pratishtha Mahotsav*, organized by the Shri Todarmal Smarak Trust in February 2012. Upon the arrival of the altar and the images in Dallas, a three-day altar Pratishtha Mahotsav was conducted in Dallas from July 13–15, 2012, presided over by Sanjeev Godha under the guidance of Hukumchand Bharill. With the enthusiastic participation of over 500 people of all Jain traditions, the three *pratimas* were installed on the altar with joyous and devotional chants from scriptures. Additionally, in six recessed shelves, three on each side of the altar, are six Jain sacred texts installed with fully prescribed rituals. They include *Panch Paramagam*, written by Acharya Kundkund, *Samayasāra, Pravachanasāra, Niyamasāra, Panchāstikāya, Ashtapāhuda*, and *Pshatkhandagama*, written by Āchārya Pushpadant and Bhutbali.

The adjoining temple, named Shree Dharamnātha Śvetāmbara Jinālaya, built in the Śvetāmbara tradition, has a Lord Parshvanath image, from the Apollo Center, facing North. With the guidance of Acharya Jayghoshsuri and Acharya Rajyashsuri, it was decided to install Lord Dharamnath as *Mulnayak*. Three additional images were installed of Lord Mahavira, Lord Adinath, and Lord Munisuvratnath. *Pratishtha Mahotsav* for the *Panch*

Parmeshthi was celebrated in 2013. The longer-term goal is to build a larger *shikharbandhi* traditional temple.

The first Sunday of the month is reserved for rituals in the Digambara tradition and the fourth Sunday in the month for the Śvetāmbara rituals. The second Sunday is reserved for *Samayika* and board meetings (at staggered time slots) and the third Sunday for a general meeting. Every Sunday, all these activities are preceded by Pathshala classes. There are six different Pathshala classes with an overall student count of approximately 280. In addition, there are a number of very active Swadhyaya groups, which are open to members at their own convenience. In order to aid the advancement of these self-study groups, JSNT has welcomed scholarly dignitaries. Additionally, with an active Jain Youth Group and an enthusiastic Senior Forum, JSNT continues to try to strike a balance between the spiritual and socio-cultural needs of its members. With over 400 families on its roster and the uniquely high growth rate of the North Texas region, JSNT is one of the most progressive and vibrant Jain organizations in the United States. The Society continues to be generously supported by its members and owns the 5.6-acre land in Garland on which *"Charan Padukas"* (footprints of Jain Tirthankaras) were installed in December 2011 as a symbolic extension of JSNT. With the influx of a large number of Jains since 2010, the community leaders are now looking for a larger property to build a larger temple with ongoing negotiations to sell off the Garland property.

Appendix 2
Jain Diaspora

Cromwell Crawford

Jains of the world, come and hear
Diaspora is here, you have nothing to fear.
From Mumbai to Mombasa, Mid pleasures and palaces, wherever
you roam, you have a place to call your home.
Ahimsa makes us one, we adore it with Tan, Man, and Dhan.
Blessed be the ties that bind our lives in kindred love.
A joy like which is only found in heaven above.
We share each other's joys, each other's burdens bear,
And often for each other flows a sympathetic tear.
So, praise the visionaries who brought us here ... guiding lights of
Jain Diaspora!
And be of good cheer, all of you are here!
You all deserve our praise, in men like you our future lies.
Each Jain is also a conqueror. That's what unifies us in Diaspora.
Jai Jinendra Bolo ... heart and mind Kholo.
Our mission is to disperse, and never cease,
Bhagvan Mahavir's message of non-killing and peace,
And to shine like jewels in a dark world,
Until it is filled with his glory as the waters cover the seas.

Appendix 3
Jain temples in North America

Canada

Alberta

Jain Society of Alberta

14225–133 Avenue
Edmonton, AB T5L 4W3
Tel: 780-435-9070

British Columbia

Jain Center of British Columbia

Unit 208
14770, 64 Avenue
Surrey, BC V3S 1X7
Tel: 604-639-5246
www.jaincenterbc.org
info@jaincenterbc.org

Ontario

Adinatha Swamy Jain Temple

7875 Mayfield Road
Brampton, ON L7E 0W1
Tel: 416-469-1109
info@jaintemplecanada.com

Jain Society of Toronto

48 Rosemeade Avenue

Etobicoke, ON M8Y 3A5
Tel: 416-251-8112
www.jsotcanada.org
info@jsotcanada.org

Jain Association of Ottawa – Carleton

3 Huntwood Ct.
Ottawa, ON K1V 0R3
Tel: 613-736-0783

Jain Samaj of Niagara Falls – Canada

Pen Centre R.P.O.
St. Catharines, ON L2T 4C4
Tel: 905-356-7575
www.niagarahindusamaj.org
info@niagarahindusamaj.org

Quebec

Montreal Jain Association

1830 Boulevard Edouard Laurin
Montreal, QC H4L 2C2
Tel: 514-747-9707

United States

Arizona

Jain Center of Greater Phoenix

6250 S 23rd Ave
Phoenix, AZ 85041
Tel: 623-334-2836
www.jcgp.org
jain_phoenix@hotmail.com

California

Jain Center of S. California – Los Angeles

8072 Commonwealth Ave
Buena Park, CA 90621

Tel: 714-523-5246
www.jaincenter.org
JCSC.Connect@gmail.com

Jain Society of Greater Sacramento

8360 Sheldon Road
Elk Grove, CA 95624
Tel: 916-635-2521
www.jcgsac.org
jainsac@hotmail.com

Jain Center of Northern California

722 South Main Street
Milpitas, CA 95035
Tel: 408-262-6242
www.jcnc.org
info@jcnc.org

Jain Society of San Diego

1830 Anna Lane
Vista, CA 92083
Tel: 760-440-5246
www.jssd.org
donations@jssd.org

Colorado

Jain Center of Colorado

10976 West 66th Ave
Arvada, CO 80004
Tel: 303-420-7049
www.jainsamajofcolorado.org
jsoc@jainsamajofcolorado.org

Connecticut

Jain Center of Connecticut

7 Trailing Ridge Rd.
Brookfield, CT 06804
Tel: 203-775-1906

www.jaincenterofconnecticut.org
jaincenterconnecticut@gmail.com

Jain Center of Greater Hartford

23 Fellen Road
Storrs, CT 06268
Tel: 860-487-0607

Florida

Jain Society of Central Florida

407 W Citrus Street
Altamonte Springs, FL 32714
Tel: 321-773-9974
www.jsocf.org
president@jsocf.org

Jain Center of Ft. Myers

6759 Highland Pines Cir.
Fort Myers, FL 33966
Tel: 239-561-2731

Jain Association of Northeast Florida

4968 Greenland Road
Jacksonville, FL 32258
Tel: 904-268-7631
www.jaxjaintemple.org
jaxjanef@gmail.com

Shree Mahavir Jain Sangh

11000 Front Beach Road
Panama City Beach, FL 32407
Tel: 850-319-5060

Jain Society Inc. of Tampa Bay

5511-A Lynn Road
Tampa, FL 33624
Tel: 813-962-0006
www.jainsocietytampabay.org

info@jainsocietytampabay.org

Jain Association of Palm Beach &Treasure Coast

3949 Whaleboat Way
Wellington, FL 33414
Tel: 561-793-3564

Jain Center of South Florida

1960 N. Commerce Parkway #11
Weston, FL 33326
Tel: 954-778-2906
www.jaincentersfl.org
Jain_Center_sfl@yahoo.com

Jain Vishwa Bharati

7819 Lillwill Ave
Orlando, FL 32809
www.JainVishwaBharati.org
info@jainvishwabharati.org

Georgia

Augusta Jain Community

408 Hastings Place
Martinez, GA 30907
Tel: 706-863-6976
www.augustahts.org

Jain Society of Greater Atlanta

669 South Peachtree Street
Norcross, GA 30071
Tel: 770-807-6187
www.jsgatemple.org
ec@jsgatemple.org

Illinois

Jain Society of Metro Chicago

435 North Route 59

Bartlett, IL 60103
Tel: 630-837-1077
www.jsmconline.org
info@myjsmc.org

Kansas

Jain Association of Kansas City

15404 W 79th Terrace
Lenexa, KS 66219
Tel: 913-383-2293
kcjainsangh@yahoogroups.com

Kentucky

Jain Center of Louis Ville

507 Bedford Shine Road
Louis Ville KY 50222
Tel: 502-426-8658

Louisiana

Jain Society of Southern Louisiana

3829 Deer Creek Lane
Harvey, LA 70058
Tel: 504-340-4283

Maryland

Jain Society of Metro Washington

1021 Briggs Chaney Road
Silver Spring, MD 20905
Tel: 301-236-4466
www.jainsocietydc.com
Webmaster@JainSocietyDC.org

Massachusetts

Jain Center of Greater Boston

556 Nichols Street

Norwood, MA 02062
Tel: 781-762-9490
www.jcgb.org
treasurer@jcgb.org

Jain Sangh of New England

223 Middlesex Turnpike
Burlington, MA 01803
Tel: 781-221-7864
www.jsne.org
webmaster@jsne.org

Michigan

Jain Society of Greater Lansing

1047 Prescott Dr.
East Lansing, MI 48823
Tel: 517-347-4168

Jain Society of Greater Detroit

29278 W 12 Mile Road
Farmington Hills, MI 48334
Tel: 248-851-5246
www.jsgd.org
jsgd-subscribe@yahoogroups.com

Minnesota

Jain Center of Minnesota

10530 Troy Ln N
Maple Grove, MN 55311
Tel: 952-402-0543
www.jaincentermn.org
Jain.Center.MN@Gmail.com

Missouri

Jain Center of Greater St. Louis

725 Weidman Rd
Saint Louis, MO 63011

Tel: 636-225-0485
www.jcstl.org
jcstl.mail@gmail.com

Nevada

Jain Society of Las Vegas

1701 Sageberry Drive
Las Vegas, NV 89144
Tel: 702-304-9207
www.hindutemplelv.org
contactus@hindutemplelv.org

New Jersey

Jain Samaj of USA

538–540 52nd St
West New York, NJ 07093
Tel: 201-330-0115
www.jsou.org

International Jain Sangh

3 Deerpath Drive
Farmingdale, NJ 07727
Tel: 732-493-0093
www.ijsonline.org
internationaljainsangh@yahoo.com

Delaware Jain Sangh

3401 Cooper Ave.
Pennsauken, NJ 08109
Tel: 856-662-2627

Jain Sangh of N.J. – Cherry Hill

3401 Cooper Ave
Pennsauken Township, NJ 08109
Tel: 856-912-0823
www.jainsangh.org
Jainsanghcherryhill@gmail.com

Jain Sangh of Atlantic City

571 South Pomona Road
Pomona, NJ 08215
Tel: 609-965-1348
www.achindutemple.org

Jain Center of NJ – Franklin Township

111 Cedar Grove Lane
Somerset, NJ 08873
Tel: 732-455-2652
www.jaincenternj.org
info@jaincenternj.org

Jain Center of NJ – Caldwell

233 Runnymede Road
Essex Fells, NJ 07021
Tel: 973-226-2539
www.jaincenternj.org
info@jaincenternj.org

Jain Vishwa Bharati of North America

151 Middlesex Ave
Iselin, NJ 08830
Tel: 732-404-1430
www.jvbnewjersey.org
info@jvbnj.org

New York

Jain Center of Syracuse

3023 Brickwalk Way
Baldwinsville, NY 13027
Tel: 315-622-3287

Jain Community of Buffalo

1071 Ransom Rd.
Grand Island, NY 14072
Tel: 716-774-8143

Jain Association of Elmira

108 Lincoln Road
Horseheads, NY 14845
Tel: 607-796-9065

Jain Society of Capitol District – Albany

16 Omega Terrace
Latham, NY 12110
Tel: 518-377-2100
albanyhindutemple@gmail.com

Jain Society of Rochester

2171 Monroe County Line Road
Macedon, NY 14502
Tel: 716-377-2100

Greater Binghamton Jain Sangh

505 African Road
Vestal, NY 13850
Tel: 607-754-6010

Jain Sangh of Hudson Valley

3 Brown Road
Wappingers Falls, NY 12590
Tel: 845-297-9061
hindusamajtemple@gmail.com

Jain Center of America – NY

43-11 Ithaca Street
Elmhurst, NY 11373
Tel: 718-478-9141
www.nyjaincenter.org
Info@NYJainCenter.org

Jain Meditation International Center

401 E 86th Street #1
New York, NY 10028

Phone 212-534-6090
www.JainMeditation.org

Jain Society of Long Island

11 Wilshire Lane
Plainview, NY 11803
Phone 516-827-0010
www.JainSamajOfLI.org

North Carolina

Jain Center of Greater Charlotte

7631 Mallard Creek Road
Charlotte, NC 28262
Tel: 704-921-1464
www.jaincenter.us
info@jaincenter.us

Jain Study Center of N. Carolina – Raleigh

509 Carriage Woods Circle
Raleigh, NC 27607
Tel: 919-859-4994
www.jscnc.org
jscnc101@gmail.com

Ohio

Jain Center of Cincinnati/Dayton

6798 Cincinnati Dayton Road
Liberty Township, OH 45044
Tel: 513-290-4002
www.jccinday.com
info@jccinday.com

Jain Center of Central Ohio – Columbus

6683 South Old State Rd.
Lewis Center, OH 43035
Tel: 513-290-7424
www.jcoco.org

Jain Society of Greater Cleveland

3226 Boston Mills Road
Richfield, OH 44286
Tel: 330-659-0832
www.jsgc.org
jsgc09@gmail.com

Jain Center of Toledo

4336 King Road
Sylvania, OH 43560
Tel: 419-843-4440

Oklahoma

Tulsa Jain Sangh

6922 South Utica
Tulsa, OK 74136
Tel: 918-369-3163

Oregon

Jain Society of Oregon

5432 SW Seymour Street
Portland, OR 97221
Tel: 503-292-1965

Pennsylvania

Philadelphia Jain Sangh of Samarpan Temple

6515 Bustleton Ave
Philadelphia, PA 19149
Tel: 215-537-9537
www.samarpantemple.org
pujari@samarpantemple.org

Samarpan Jain Sangh

9701 Bustleton Ave
Philadelphia, PA 19149
Tel: 215-464-7676

Jain Center of Allentown

4200 Airport Road
Allentown, PA 18109
Tel: 610-868-1231
www.hindutempleallentown.org

Jain Sangh of North East PA

601 Hampton Rd
Shavertown, PA 18708
Tel: 570-696-2202
Arihant101@yahoo.com

Jain Society of Pittsburgh

615 Illini Drive
Monroeville, PA 15146
Tel: 724-325-2073
www.hindujaintemple.org

Jain Center of South-Central PA

301 Steigerwalt Hollow Rd
New Cumberland, PA 17070
Tel: 717-774-6746

Samarpan Jain Sangh

9701 Bustleton Avenue
Philadelphia, PA 19115
Tel: 215-464-7676

Samarpan Jain Sangh – Hindu Temple

6515 Bustleton Avenue
Philadelphia, PA 19149
Tel: 215-537-9537
www.samarpantemple.org
pujari@samarpantemple.org

Tennessee

Jain Society of Middle Tennessee

2273 Dewitt Dr.
Clarksville, TN 37043
Tel: 931-648-9535

Jain Society of Greater Memphis

2173 East Glenalden Drive
Germantown, TN 38139
Tel: 901-757-4948

Texas

Jain Society of North Texas

11321 Webb Chapel Road
Dallas, TX 75220
Tel: 972-359-1863
www.dfwjains.org
info@jsnt.org

Jain Center of West Texas

1110 Juneau Ave
Lubbock, TX 79416
Tel: 409-295-1600

Jain Sangh of Greater Austin

1600 Iris Ln
Cedar Park, TX 78613
Tel: 512-250-5385
www.jainsanghofgreateraustin.org
austinjainparivar@yahoogroups.com

JVB Preksha Meditation Center

14102 Schiller Rd
Houston, TX 77082
Tel: 281-596-9642
www.jvbhouston.org
info@jvbhouston.org

Jain Society of Houston

    3905 Arc Street
    Houston, TX 77063
    Tel: 713-789-2338
    www.jainsocietyhouston.org
    info@jsh-houston.org

Virginia

Jain Temple of Virginia

    3656 Centerview Dr Unit 5
    Chantilly, VA 20151
    Tel: 571-299-6688
    www.jaintempleva.org
    contact@jaintempleva.org

Richmond Jain Society of Virginia

    6051 Springfield Road
    Glen Allen, VA 23060
    Tel: 804-364-1428
    www.jsrva.org
    info@jsrva.org

Wisconsin

Jain Center of Wisconsin

    N4063 W243 Pewaukee Rd
    Highway 164 N
    Pewaukee, WI 53072
    Tel: 262-242-4827
    www.jainwi.org
    Jaintemplewis@hotmail.com

Appendix 4

List of universities offering Jain Studies

Sulekh Jain

Table A.1 List of universities offering Jain Studies

No.	Year established	Location	Title	Professor/Fellow
1	2004	India and the USA	International School for Jain Studies	Attended by 700+ participants so far
2	2010	Florida International University, Miami, FL	Bhagwan Mahavir Professorship in Jain Studies	Dr. Steven Vose, Bhagwan Mahavir Assistant Professor of Jain Studies
3	2012–2014	Claremont Lincoln University, Claremont, CA	Postdoctoral Fellow	Professor Philip Clayton and Dr. Brianne Donaldson
4	2015	University of California, Irvine, CA	Shri Bhagwan Parshvanath Presidential Chair in Jain Studies	Position not yet filled
5	2015	Emory University, Atlanta, GA	Jain Studies in the Dept. of South Asian Religion	Dr. Ellen Gough, Assistant Professor
6	2016–2018	Loyola Marymount University, Los Angeles, CA	50% Jain, 50% Sikh Professorship	Professor Nirinjan Khalsa
7	2016	University of North Texas, Denton, TX	Bhagwan Adinath Professorship in Jain Studies	Dr. George James
8	2016	Rice University, Houston, TX	Bhagwan Mahavir and Chao Foundation Post-doctoral Fellowship	Dr. Brianne Donaldson
9	2016	Claremont School of Theology, Claremont, CA	Graduate Course in Jain Studies	Professor Shushma Parekh
10	2017	University of California, Davis, CA	Mohini Jain Presidential Chair in Jain Studies	Position not yet filled
11	2017	University of California, Riverside, CA	Shrimad Rajchandra Endowed Chair in Jain Studies	Professor Dr. Ana Bajzelj

No.	Year established	Location	Title	Professor/Fellow
12	2017	Loyola Marymount University, Los Angeles, CA	Bhagwan Mallinath Professorship in Jain Studies	Position not yet filled
13	2018	University of California, Santa Barbara, CA	Bhagwan Vimalnath Lectureship in Jain Studies	Position not yet filled
14	2018	California State University Fullerton, CA	Bhagwan Shantinath Program in Jain Studies	Position not yet filled
15	2018	California State University, Northridge, CA	Bhagwan Ajitnath Endowed Professorship in Jain Studies	Position not yet filled
16	2019	San Diego State University, San Diego, CA	Bhagwan Sumatinath and Guru Nanak Post-doctoral Fellowship in Jain and Sikh Studies	Position not yet filled

Source: Sulekh Jain.

Appendix 5
A brief art history of Jain sculpture in North America

On March 30, 1971, *The New York Times* published an obituary for one of the world's leading art collectors, Nasli Heeramaneck.[1] Heeramaneck was born into a Zoroastrian family of an art dealer in Mumbai and migrated to the USA in 1927. With his wife, Alice Heeramaneck, he collected many Indian works of art that he donated to various American and Indian museums from time to time. They had three Jain statues in their possession. One of them was a ninth-century image of the 23rd Jain Tirthankara Lord Parshvanath (Sharma 1976). An exquisite image, perhaps from the eleventh century, Bihar, of Lord Parshvanath is also in the Avery Brundage Collection. Another image, also of Lord Parshvanath, is in the Cleveland Museum of Art. That piece may be from tenth-century Central India.

The Jason B. Grossman Collection had a tenth-century piece from Rajasthan, depicting the head of a Jina. Another piece from ninth-century Central India was seen in the collection of Harry Lenart. In Boston Art Museum, a tenth-century image from North India is of the first Jain Tirthankara Lord Adinath. Here, a bronze statue from Mysore, dating from the ninth or tenth century, is also found. In the Philadelphia Museum of Art, an eleventh-century stone statue, from Chola times, of another Tirthankara is present. This piece was obtained in exchange from Delhi's National Museum. A similar bronze statue from Rajasthan or Gujarat, dating from approximately the tenth century, is found in the Anjali Gallery. Los Angeles County Museum of Art has a display of Lord Vimalnath (sixteenth century). A stone statue from Odisha, dating from the tenth century, of the Jain goddess Ambika is displayed in the Stendhal Gallery. Also in the Avery Brundage Collection is a stone statue of the goddess, obtained from Jhansi, Uttar Pradesh, and may date from the eleventh century, an example of Chandel art. Two tenth- or eleventh-century bronze statues of the Jain goddess were obtained from Mysore and are now displayed in Boston Art Museum. A fourteenth-century brass statue from Western India is present in the Anjali Gallery. Similarly, a sixteenth-century Jain shrine that was acquired in 1932 was finally curated in 2002 at the Nelson-Atkins Museum of Art in Kansas City.

Jain art history has periodically been exhibited in various museum shows and exhibitions across America. In 2009, in New York,[2] two shows, "Victorious

Ones: Jain Images of Perfection" and "Peaceful Conquerors: Jain Manuscript
Painting," at the Rubin Museum of Art and at the Metropolitan Museum of
Art, respectively, focused on Jain art history. In 1986, the New York Public
Library displayed Jain manuscripts in an exhibition called "The World of Jain-
ism."[3] According to Robert Del Bonta, the Boston Museum of Fine Art, Yale
University Museum, the Virginia Museum of Fine Arts, Berkeley Art Museum,
and the Los Angeles County Museum of Art also have significant Jain materials.

Notes

1 See www.nytimes.com/1971/03/30/archives/nasli-m-heeramaneck-dead-dealer-in-asia
n-art-objects.html (accessed May 18, 2019).
2 See www.nytimes.com/slideshow/2009/11/13/arts/20091113-jain_index.html (accessed May 18, 2019).
3 John Russell, "Art: Exhibition of Indian Manuscripts at Library," *The New York
Times*, August 29, 1986. Available at: https://libproxy.library.unt.edu:6570/api/docum
ent?collection=news&id=urn:contentItem:3S8G-9D70-0007-H2HG-00000-00&con
text= 1516831 (accessed May 18, 2019).

Appendix 6
An interview about celebrating Asian holidays in Texas public schools

In August 2017, we met the Coppell ISD superintendent to request considering making Diwali a holiday, as a professional development day for Coppell ISD students and then the www.change.org petition was created. It has now gathered almost 1,750 signatures, all across Coppell ISD people have signed it. It requests considering Diwali as a professional development day, not as a holiday, but as a staff development day or professional development day.

Q: Okay. Why do you think we need such kind of petitions in each school?

A: Right, so I came to this country in 1996. We were in New Jersey. New Jersey is where this has already happened, so more than six, seven, eight school districts across New Jersey, across New York also six or seven school districts, one in Pennsylvania, Maryland, Massachusetts, so almost 20 school districts in the Northeast have already declared Diwali as a professional development day and also the Chinese New Year and also Eid. So these three holidays, all these school districts have accepted them, to acknowledge the Asian demographics in their school districts. Asian students are a significant number, so these holidays have been added in New Jersey, New York, and elsewhere. With Coppell ISD's high numbers, almost 50 percent of the students are of Asian heritage. When you say Asian heritage, they are mostly of Indian heritage, technically speaking, so it should be, you know, we are just following what other states have done in this country, not looking at India. We are American citizens here. What other American states have done, maybe something similar can be done in Texas as well.

Q: Okay, but with this petition, what kind of support did you expect from the community and what is it that you got?

A: Right. That is a great question. When we started the petition, we didn't imagine what would happen, I mean, we couldn't imagine, but this, I'm really very fortunate, very happy, very blessed to say that we have 1,750 signatures almost. Community has [helped], I think many of us are still new to the country. We don't even realize what rights we have, already possible in this country, what are our responsibilities and rights toward our school system, what we can do and what is possible under the

American Constitution, Texas State Laws, and School District Laws, what is possible, that awareness is spreading like wildfire because of the petition, because of the two election runs that we had, Vara and I, your friend, we both ran, you know, year by year.

Q: Okay.

A: First, I did, then Vara did, and then this petition came. These are not the moves for any political games. There is no possibility of political games. I'm an educator, I'm a researcher of culture, I'm an anthropologist, I'm a parent, right? So that is what is driving me to do these things and to raise awareness. So in terms of awareness in Coppell ISD, it doesn't matter whether they are Indian or non-Indian, every person in Coppell ISD knows what Diwali is, how Diwali is celebrated. We took the Coppell ISD staff superintendent and directors and principals to the temple, the BAPS Temple, last Diwali. It is an amazing success of awareness. Everybody knows now just like Christians have a holiday for Christmas, we all celebrate that. We celebrate Halloween, we celebrate Thanksgiving, right? Easter, we celebrate. Now we need to celebrate Diwali also with equal interest, equal passion, and we need to tell our teachers, we need to tell our colleagues and friends that Diwali is as important if not less. It is as important as Christmas, New Year, and Thanksgiving, if we combine all that into one festival.

Q: But considering that, more or less, we don't talk about the next generation that was born here, but when we talk about ourselves, we are all immigrants and we are in this new land. Aren't these kind of petitions making us uncomfortable living in this country. because definitely the other cultures might look at us in a different way, asking why these people coming from other countries are trying to push their culture on us?

A: Right. It is a long-term visionary step that we need to take as parents and taxpayers in the Coppell ISD. Coppell ISD, as you know, is one of the highest property tax school districts. The reason it has such a high property tax is because the school system is so good, right? To maintain the quality of the school system, we all work very hard, parents work very hard, students work very hard. Now in addition to acknowledging the diversity of the school population, the student population, what are the ways that are not just for our generation, but what are the ways that our culture can be safeguarded for all future generations? This can be one humble step to start with. It is not the end, but it is a start, so Diwali should be acknowledged more. What other things can be done to make sure that nobody, no student born in this country feels that he or she is oppressed, he or she is bullied, there should not be any discrimination? How can we make sure that we have this great opportunity where such a diverse group of students are present in Coppell ISD, Plano ISD, Frisco ISD, what we can do to make sure that North Texas truly emerges as a truly pluralistic community where every culture is respected, all festivals are celebrated equally, and everybody feels welcomed, truly welcomed? It shouldn't be just a hollow slogan. Diversity is not just a hollow slogan, we need to really embrace the diversity, we need to practice what we preach.

Q: Okay. So, do you think this petition that you filed was filed quite early? Maybe you could have taken another couple of years and you would have got more support to get it approved or something like that?

A: As I told you, there are 1,750 signatures. I'm a researcher. I have looked at the petitions for Diwali in New York, New Jersey. None of the places got even 500 signatures and it was approved. Here we have 1,750 signatures, and here it will take time, I guess, the culture is a little bit different in Texas compared to New York and New Jersey, but somewhere, somebody has to start, take a first step. It will take a few years. Even in New York, in New Jersey, it took three years, four years, to make it happen. Nothing happens overnight. It is a start, it is a great start. Everybody knows now about Diwali, what Diwali is and it is a very, very important festival for our community and for every community now. So it is a start, and somebody somewhere has to start. The idea came to me when I was writing, I'm still writing my book on the history of Hindus in North and South America.

Q: Okay.

A: Did you know that in Suriname, Trinidad and Tobago and other Caribbean countries, Diwali is a national holiday? With only 25 percent Hindus, there is a national holiday for Diwali. Suriname is a country in South America where Hindi is spoken, now those Indians, those Hindus came to those countries about 150 years ago, but they kept their language alive, they kept their festivals alive, so the future generations can still celebrate. It is a national holiday with only 25 percent of the population. Coppell ISD has almost 50 percent student population with that heritage, why can't we dedicate just one day when we have other festivals? We celebrate Good Friday, we celebrate Christmas, there are holidays for those festivals, why not Diwali?

Q: Okay. So definitely the petition that you filed may take a while, but you have been standing in elections in Coppell School District.

A: Just one, just once.

Q: Yeah.

A: Never again. I'm not going to run again.

Q: Okay.

A: I'm not a politician, I did that also for the first year just to make people aware that this is possible. It is possible to join the school board. See, as I said, we have to learn from other cultures, other immigrant groups. Latinos in our neighboring districts, Grand Prairie, Irving, Flower Mound and other places, everywhere there is a Latino on the school board. How did it happen? It does not happen miraculously, right? People work for it. People file lawsuits. Every school district, every city council, including Irving, where we are sitting right now, Latinos have filed lawsuits against the city councils and against school boards to make sure that the voting system is reformed. Right now, the election system is "at large," what is called "at large." Now "at large" was reformed because of these lawsuits and "at large" was divided into sub-districts, so wherever Latinos are in majority, one person from Latino background, preferably he or she runs and Latinos vote for him or her and that's how Latinos are in all these school districts. So this is exactly what we need, I think. In the long term, maybe without the lawsuit probably, it is not the best way to go. I mean, we are not into confrontation, and so on, but unless we have our own representation in city councils and our school boards, it is a possibility at least, so by my running in 2016, there was this awareness that somebody can actually join the school board for Coppell ISD, Plano ISD, Frisco ISD, and can, you know, make sure that all cultures are treated with respect and equality and mutual trust. That is worth the effort.

Q: So what is your vision and goal for Coppell ISD in future? Do you want to be part of it and do something for the community?

A: I will remain a professor. I will remain a researcher. I will remain a parent for many years still because my younger son is still in fifth grade, so I will be here forever.

Q: Okay.

A: So my goal is simple, like all parents I want all of our kids to gain good education, of course from Coppell ISD, which we are already getting. Coppell ISD is a great school system, but we also need to share our culture with all our humility. The kids should be proud of their heritage. This is the heritage that gave us Mahatma Gandhi. Mahatma Gandhi gave nonviolence to Dr. Martin Luther King. Dr. Martin Luther King's civil rights movement was launched after he went to India. Dr. King actually visited the home of Mahatma Gandhi in Mumbai and he came back and he launched the civil rights movement. Because of his work, immigration laws were changed and we are here. Otherwise, we would not even be included. Did you know that in 1923, Indian citizens were robbed of their citizenships? Citizenship was taken back from Indians and they were deported. Even citizens in 1923, and in 1965, the laws were changed eventually and eventually the laws were relaxed and Asian people could come to this country again. Otherwise, they were prohibited. So we are all grateful to Dr. King's battles. Because of that, we are here and we need to continue to, you know, request all civil rights. All cultures should be treated with mutual trust and respect.

Q: It was nice talking to you about this, but definitely there was a small step back with the refusal of Coppell ISD to make a holiday on Diwali. I hope this tradition or trend will keep coming up in coming years where you will again request this to the board, but what is your final take on the refusal and then your conclusion?

A: Yeah, this refusal is just a start. As I said, even New York, New Jersey, took three years to make it happen, so we have right now petitions going on for Diwali as a Professional Day for Coppell ISD, Plano ISD, Frisco ISD, Allen ISD, Southlake ISD, and Lewisville ISD. So whoever is living in those areas, please go to change.org website, Google "Coppell Diwali change.org," "Lewisville Diwali change.org," "Frisco Diwali change.org," "Plano Diwali change.org," "Southlake Diwali change.org," and "Allen Diwali change.org." Please sign those petitions in your respective neighborhoods and please spread the word. This is nothing, you know, there is nothing drastic or radical that we are asking. We are only asking what has already happened in New York, New Jersey, Maryland, Pennsylvania, and Massachusetts. Nothing different we are asking, so please, you know, sign the petitions, spread the word, and please go to those board meetings in your respective school districts, and request your board members to recognize a very valid request, a very legitimate request, because we are taxpayers and we make the school district run and we are only requesting equality for all cultures. Nothing radical, nothing different.

Bibliography

Abrahams, Ruth K. "The Life and Art of Uday Shankar," unpublished PhD dissertation, New York University, 1986.

Ainouche, Linda. *Dreadlocks Story*, 2017. Documentary. Available at: www.gold.ac. uk/calendar/?id=11065

Algoe, Rishmidevi K. "Institutional Development of Christianity, Hinduism, and Islam in Suriname and Trinidad: An Exploration in Religious Practice and Festivities from 1900–2010," *Academic Journal of Suriname* 2(2011): 186–197.

Altman, Michael J. "The Construction of Hinduism in America," *Religion Compass* 10(8) (2016): 207–216,

Altman, Michael J. *Heathen, Hindoo, Hindu: American Representations of India, 1721–1893*. Oxford: Oxford University Press, 2017.

Arnold, Alison. "Music and Internationalization," in *The Garland Encyclopedia of World Music: South Asia: The Indian Subcontinent*. Oxford: Garland, 2015, pp. 586–597.

Arya, Usharbudh. *Ritual Songs and Folksongs of the Hindus of Surinam*. Leiden: Brill, 1968.

Aukland, Knut. "The Scientization and Academization of Jainism," *Journal of the American Academy of Religion* 84(1) (2016): 192–233.

Backman, Michael. "Diamonds, Jains, and Jews," in *Inside Knowledge: Streetwise in Asia*. Basingstoke: Palgrave Macmillan, 2005, pp. 160–166.

Bald, Vie. *Bengali Harlem and the Lost Histories of South Asian America*. Cambridge, MA: Harvard University Press, 2015.

Beck, Guy L. "Kirtan and Bhajan in Bhakti Traditions," in Knut A. Jacobsen (Ed.), *Brill's Encyclopedia of Hinduism*, vol. II. Leiden: Brill Academic Publishers, 2010, pp. 585–598.

Beck, Guy L. "Hinduism," in Charles Hiroshi Garrett (Ed.), *The Grove Dictionary of American Music*, 2nd ed., vol. IV. New York: Oxford University Press, 2013, pp. 173–174.

Bentley, William. *The Diary of William Bentley, Pastor of the East Church, Salem, Massachusetts*. Gloucester, MA: Smith, [1905], 1962.

Bhalla, Vibha. "'We Wanted to End Disparities at Work': Physician Migration, Racialization, and a Struggle for Equality," *Journal of American Ethnic History* 29(3) (2010): 40–78.

Bhatt, Kanti. "Mafat Kaka, India's Diamond Trade Pioneer," *Rediff.com*. September 14, 2005.

Bilefsky, Dan. "Indians Unseat Antwerp's Jews as the Biggest Diamond Traders: Lower-Cost Production in Bombay, Gujarat Has Facilitated the Change," *The Wall Street Journal*, May 27, 2003.

Blavatsky, Helena P. *Isis Unveiled*. Pasadena, CA: Theosophical Society Press, 1877.

Blume, Gernot. "Blurred Affinities: Tracing the Influence of North Indian Classical Music in Keith Jarrett's Solo Piano Improvisations," *Popular Music*, 22(2) (2003): 117–142.

Bowe, Kyle Patrick. "(R)evolution of Self: An Ethnographic Investigation into the Stratums of Inspiration in the Rhythms of Yoga and Music," MA thesis, San Diego State University, 2016.

Bourke-White, Margaret. *Halfway to Freedom: A Report on the New India in the Words and Photographs of Margaret Bourke-White*. New York: Simon & Schuster, 1949, pp. 225–233.

Brettell, Caroline and Deborah Reed-Danahay. *Civic Engagements: The Citizenship Practices of Hindu and Vietnamese Immigrants*. Redwood City, CA: Stanford University Press, 2011.

Brown, Emily C. *Har Dayal, Hindu Revolutionary and Rationalist*. New Delhi: Manohar, 1976.

Brown, Sara Black. "'Every Word Is a Song, Every Step Is a Dance': Participation, Agency, and the Expression of Communal Bliss in Hare Krishna Festival Kirtan," PhD dissertation. Florida State University, 2012.

Brown, Sara Black. "Krishna, Christians, and Colors: The Socially Binding Influence of Kirtan Singing at a Utah Hare Krishna Festival," *Ethnomusicology* 58(3) (2014): 454–480.

Buettner, Elizabeth. "'Going for an Indian': South Asian Restaurants and the Limits of Multiculturalism in Britain," *Journal of Modern History* 80 (2008): 865–901.

Burg van der, Cors and Peter van der Veer. "Pandits, Profit, and Power: Religious Organization and the Construction of Identity among Surinamese Hindus," *Ethnic and Racial Studies* 9(4) (1986).

Burgess, Vincent E. "Indian Influences on Rastafarianism," Honors thesis, Ohio State University, 2007.

Chakravorty, Sanjoy, Devesh Kapur, and Nirvikar Singh. *The Other One Percent: Indians in America*. New York, NY: Oxford University Press, 2017.

Chatterji, Priya. "Indian Classical Music," *East and West* 8(4) (1958): 360–370.

Chetana, Florida Catherine. "Guidelines for Initiation Provided by Gurudev Chitrabhanu," *The Lighthouse Beacon* 48, Summer/Fall (2006).

Choenni, Chan E. S. "Hindostanis in Suriname, 1873–1920: Indenture, Plantations and Beyond," *Nidān: International Journal for Indian Studies* 1(1) (2016): 48–84.

Clarke, Colin. *East Indians in a West Indian Town. San Fernando, Trinidad, 1930–1970*. London: Allen and Unwin, 1986.

Clarke, Colin, "Society and Electoral Politics in Trinidad and Tobago," in Colin Clarke (Ed.), *Society and Politics in the Caribbean*. London: St Antony's/Macmillan, 1991, pp. 47–77.

Clarke, Colin. "Spatial Pattern and Social Interaction among Creoles and Indians in Trinidad and Tobago," in Kevin Yelvington (Ed.), *Trinidad Ethnicity*. London: Warwick Macmillan Caribbean Studies, 1993, pp. 116–135.

Cockrell, Eddie. "Film Review: 'For Here or to Go?'" *Variety*, March 29, 2017. Available at: http://variety.com/2017/film/reviews/for-here-or-to-go-film-review-1202019219/

Cooke, Jubilee Q. "Kirtan in Seattle: New Hootenanny for Spirit Junkies," PhD dissertation, University of Washington, 2009.

Corrigan, John, and Winthrop S. Hudson. *Religion in America*. New York: Routledge, 2018.

Costain, Balabhadra Bruce. *Applied Jainism*. Nashville, TN: Omni PublishXpress, 2003.

Dadabhoy, Bakhtiar. *Zubin Mehta: A Musical Journey*. Gurgaon, India: Penguin Viking, 2016.

Das, Rajani K. *Hindustani Workers on the Pacific Coast*. Berlin: W. de Gruyter & Co, 1923.

DeSilver, Drew. "5 Facts about Indian Americans. 2014." Available at: www.pewresearch.org/fact-tank/2014/09/30/5-facts-about-indian-americans/

Dew, Anke D. *Fertility and Culture Among Hindus in Surinam*. New Haven, CT: Yale University, 1975.

Dhingra, Pawan. *Life Behind the Lobby: Indian American Motel Owners and the American Dream*. Stanford, CA: Stanford University Press, 2012.

Dixit, Balwant N. "Globalization and Indian Classical Music: The North American Scene," 2002. Available at: www.india-arts.pitt.edu/globalization.html (accessed January 9, 2018).

Dookhan, Isaac. *A Post-Emancipation History of the West Indies*. Harlow: Longman, 1989.

Dutt, Barkha. "The Kansas Shooting Teaches Indians a Few Lessons About Trump — and the United States," *The Washington Post*, March 1, 2017.

Eck, Diana L. *A New Religious America. How a "Christian Country" Has Become the World's Most Religiously Diverse Nation*. San Francisco: HarperCollins, 2001.

Elam, Daniel. "Echoes of Ghadr: Lala Har Dayal and the Time of Anticolonialism," *Comparative Studies in South Asia, Africa, and the Middle East* 34(1) (2014): 9–23.

Emerson, Ralph W. and Merton M. Sealts. *The Journals and Miscellaneous Notebooks of Ralph Waldo Emerson*, vol. 10. Cambridge, MA: Belknap Press of Harvard University Press, 1973.

Farrell, Gerry. *Indian Music and the West*. Oxford: Oxford University Press, [1997] 2004.

Ferdman, Roberto A. "Why Delicious Indian Food Is Surprisingly Unpopular in the U.S.," *Washington Post*, March 4, 2015.

Fibiger, Marianne Qvortrup. "Śrī Mātā Amṛtānandamayī Devī: The Global Worship of an Indian Female Guru," in J. Borup and M. Fibiger (Eds.), *East Spirit: Transnational Spirituality and Religious Circulation in East and West*. Leiden: Brill, 2017, pp. 80–99.

Fibiger, Marianne Qvortrup, and Sammy Bishop. 2018. "'The Hugging Guru': Amma and Transnationalism," The Religious Studies Project (Podcast Transcript). 12 November, 2018. Version 1.1. Available at: www.religiousstudiesproject.com/podcast/the-hugging-guru-amma-and-transnationalism/

Flint, Valerie I. J. *The Imaginative Landscape of Christopher Columbus*. Princeton, NJ: Princeton University Press, 2017.

Flügel, Peter. "The Invention of Jainism: A Short History of Jaina Studies," *Journal of Jaina Studies (Kyoto)* 11 (2005): 1–19.

Forsthoefel, Thomas A. and Cynthia Ann Humes (Eds.). *Gurus in America*. Albany, NY: SUNY Press, 2005.

Gandhi, V. R. "Interview," *The New York Times*, November 29, 1897.

Gleig, Ann and Lola Williamson. *Homegrown Gurus: From Hinduism in America to American Hinduism*. Albany, NY: SUNY Press, 2014.

Goldberg, Philip. *American Veda*. New York: Harmony Books, 2010.

Gower, Karla K. "Agnes Smedley: A Radical Journalist in Search of a Cause," *American Journalism* 13 (1996).

Gower, K. Karla. (n.d.) "The Hindu-German Conspiracy: An Examination of the Coverage of Indian Nationalists in Newspapers from 1915 to 1918." Available at: http://list.msu.edu/cgi-bin/wa?a3=ind9709d&L=AEJMC&E=7BIT&P=3267393& B=-&T=TEXT%2FPLAIN;%20charset=US-ASCII (accessed June 1, 2017).

Guha, Ramachandra. *How Much Should a Person Consume?: Environmentalism in India and the United States*. Berkeley, CA: University of California Press, 2006.

Haldane, David. "East Meets West as Monk Alters Indian Rules to Fit Seaside Style," *Los Angeles Times*, September 8, 1988.

Halter, Marilyn, Marilynn S. Johnson, Katheryn P. Viens, and Conrad Edick Wright. *What's New about the "New" Immigration?: Traditions and Transformations in the United States since 1965*. Basingstoke: Palgrave Macmillan, 2014.

Hartke, Kristen. "Americans Love Spices. So Why Don't We Grow Them?" *NPR*, December 26, 2017.

Helton, Tim. "Mahavira, Mohandas, and Martin: An Ancient Religion's Influence on the United States Civil Rights Movement," unpublished paper, 2007.

Helweg, Arthur W., and Usha M. Helweg. *An Immigrant Success Story: East Indians in America*. Philadelphia, PA: University of Pennsylvania Press, 1990.

Hinduism Today. "Nature's 'Hindu Temples' on View at Grand Canyon," August 2, 1987.

Hinduism Today. "Professor Deems Holland's Bhojpuri a Distinct Language," January 16, 2002.

Hinduism Today. "Indians Came to Surinam in Search of Shri Ram 130 Years Ago," June 6, 2003.

Hingrah, Pankaz Chandmal and Hiral Dholakia-Dave. "The Forgotten Gandhi," *South Asian Times*, September 5, 2012.

Humes, Cynthia Ann. "Maharishi Ayur-Veda[TM] Perfect Health[TM] through Enlightened Marketing in America," in Dagmar Wujastyk and Frederick M. Smith (Eds.), *Modern and Global Ayurveda: Pluralism and Paradigms*. Albany, NY: State University of New York Press, 2008, pp. 309–331.

Hunter, James Davison and David Franz. "Religious Pluralism and Civil Society," in Stephen R. Prothero (Ed.), *A Nation of Religions: The Politics of Pluralism in Multireligious America*. Chapel Hill, NC: University of North Carolina Press, 2006.

Hussain, Amir. *Muslims and the Making of America*. Waco, TX: Baylor University Press, 2016.

Ingraham, Christopher. "The Richest 1 Percent Now Owns More of the Country's Wealth Than At Any Time in the Past 50 Years," *Washington Post*. December 6, 2017. Available at: www.washingtonpost.com/news/wonk/wp/2017/12/06/the-richest-1-percent-now-owns -more-of-the-countrys-wealth-than-at-any-time-in-the-past-50-years/

Jain, Andrea R. *Selling Yoga: From Counterculture to Pop Culture*. New York: Oxford University Press, 2015.

Jain, Pankaj. *Dharma and Ecology of Hindu Communities: Sustenance and Sustainability*. Farnham, Surrey: Ashgate, 2011.

Jain, Pankaj. *Science and Socio-Religious Revolution in India: Moving the Mountains*. London: Routledge, 2017.

Jain, Prakash C. *Jains in India and Abroad: A Sociological Introduction*. New Delhi: International School for Jain Studies, 2011.

Jain, Ravindra K. "Freedom Denied? Indian Women and Indentureship," *Economic and Political Weekly* 21(7) (1986): 316.

Jain, Ravindra K. *Indian Communities Abroad: Themes and Literature*. New Delhi: Q Publishers & Distributors, 1993, pp. 52–57.

Jensen, Joan M. *Passage from India: Asian Indian Immigrants in North America*. New Haven, CT: Yale University Press, 1988.

Johnson, Hollis. "A Cuisine That's Been Largely Ignored for Decades Could Be the Next Big Thing in America," *Business Insider*, January 3, 2017.

Jones, Robert P. and Benjamin P. Marcus. 2019. "America's Changing Religious Landscape," in the Religious Studies Project (Podcast Transcript). 18 February 2019. Version 1.1, February 2, 2019. Available at: www.religiousstudiesproject. com/podcast/americas-changing-religious-landscape/

Joshi, Khyati Y. *New Roots in America's Sacred Ground: Religion, Race, and Ethnicity in Indian America*. New Brunswick, NJ: Rutgers University Press, 2006.

Joshi, Khyati Y. "Standing Up and Speaking Out: Hindu Americans and Christian Normativity in Metro Atlanta," in *Asian Americans in Dixie: Race and Migration in the South*. Urbana, IL: University of Illinois Press, 2013, pp. 190–215.

Joshi, Khyati Y. and Maurianne Adams. "Religious Oppression Curriculum Design," in Maurianne Adams (Ed.), *New Teaching for Diversity and Social Justice*. New York: Routledge, 2007.

Josiam, Bharath M., and Prema A. Monteiro. "Tandoori Tastes: Perceptions of Indian Restaurants in America," *International Journal of Contemporary Hospitality Management* 16(1) (2004): 18–26.

Kalra, Virinder S. "The Political Economy of the Samosa," *South Asia Research* 24(1) (2004): 21–36.

Kamath, M. V. *The United States and India, 1776–1996: The Bridge Over the River Time*. New Delhi: Indian Council for Cultural Relations, 1998.

Kaur, Valarie, Sharat Raju, Matthew R. Blute, Amandeep S. Gill, Scott Rosenblatt, and Eric Santistevan. *Divided We Fall: Americans in the Aftermath*. Documentary. Venice, CA: New Moon Productions, 2008.

Kennedy, Rozelia Maria. "A Biographical Study of Bernard LaFayette, Jr. as an Adult Educator Including the Teaching of Nonviolence Conflict Reconciliation," doctoral thesis. The University of South Florida, 2018.

Khan, Madina. "Celebrating 50 Years of The Ali Akbar College of Music," *India Currents*, February 28, 2018.

King, Mary. *Mahatma Gandhi and Martin Luther King Jr: The Power of Nonviolent Action (Cultures of Peace)*. New York: UNESCO, 1999.

Klein, Glenn. *Faceting History: Cutting Diamonds and Colored Stones.* Philadelphia, PA: Xlibris, 2005.

Kothari, Abhijit. "Mercantile Webs: Trade Community Clusters Among the Sindhis and Palanpuri Jains," PhD dissertation, Dharamsinh Desai University, India, 2009a.

Kothari, Abhijit. "From Palanpur to Antwerp: An Entrepreneurial Journey of the Palanpuri Jains," in Nina Muncherji, C. Gopalakrishnan, and Upinder Dhar (Eds.), *Partners in Success: Strategic HR and Entrepreneurship*. Ahmedabad: Institute of Management, Nirma University of Science and Technology, 2009b, pp. 475–492.

Kotkin, Joel. "The Greater India," in *Tribes: How Race, Religion, and Identity Determine Success in the New Global Economy*. New York: Random House, 1994, pp. 475–492.

Krell, Gerald, Meyer Odze, and Marvin R. Wilson. *The Asian & Abrahamic Religions: A Divine Encounter in America*. Documentary. Potomac, MD: Auteur Productions, 2011.

Kumar, Amitava. *Away: The Indian Writer as an Expatriate*. New York: Routledge, 2003.

Kumar, Bhuvanendra. "Jains and Their Religion in America: A Social Survey," *Jain Journal* 31(1) (1996a): 39–49.

Kumar, Bhuvanendra. *Jainism in America*. Mississauga, Canada: Jain Humanities Press, 1996b.

Kumar, Komal. "The Transformations and Challenges of a Jain Religious Aspirant from Layperson to Ascetic: An Anthropological Study of Shvetambar Terapanthi Female Mumukshus," 2016. Available at: https://pdfs.semanticscholar.org/c908/b7357cc3a70bdd8cd4a7641a2511295b6c5a.pdf?_ga=2.33973281.1464237850.1568593081-217876629.1568593081

Kurien, Prema. *A Place at the Multicultural Table: The Development of an American Hinduism*. New Brunswick, NJ: Rutgers, 2007.

Kyle, Patrick Bowe. "(R)evolution of Self: An Ethnographic Investigation into the Stratums of Inspiration in the Rhythms of Yoga and Music," MA thesis, San Diego State University, 2016.

Lad, Vasant. *The Doctor from India*. Zeitgeist Films, 2018.

Lakshmi, Rama. "Son Marks Martin Luther King's 1959 Visit to India," *Washington Post*, February 18, 2009.

Lal, Vinay. *The Other Indians: A Political and Cultural History of South Asians in America*. Los Angeles, CA: Asian American Studies Center Press, 2008.

Lavezzoli, Peter. *The Dawn of Indian Music in the West: The Story of the Musical Merging of East and West*. New York: Continuum, 2007.

Lessinger, Joanna. *From the Ganges to the Hudson: Indian Immigrants in New York City*. Boston: Allyn and Bacon, 1995.

Levitt, Peggy. *God Needs No Passport: Immigrants and the Changing American Religious Landscape*. New York: New Press, 2007.

Loar, Russ. "Doctor is Devoted to Religion That Inspired Gandhi," *Los Angeles Times*, June 24, 1996.

Long, Jeffery D. *Jainism: An Introduction*. London: I.B. Tauris, 2009.

Long, Jeffery D. "Indian Food in the US: 1909–1921," 2011. Available at: saada.org/tides/article/20111018–20111417.

Long, Jeffery D. *Hinduism in America: A Convergence of Worlds*. London: Bloomsbury, 2020.

Lucia, Amanda J. *Reflections of Amma: Devotees in a Global Embrace*. Berkeley, CA: University of California Press, 2014.

Mahabir, Anil. "How Differently Hinduism Developed in the Adjacent Nations of Suriname and Guyana," *Hinduism Today*, January 2001.

Mahabir, Kumar. "The Indian Diaspora in the West Indies/Caribbean: A Cultural History of Triumphs and Tribulations," unpublished paper, 2006.

Mahadeo, Cris and Kumar Mahabir. "Indians Came to the Caribbean before Columbus," paper presented at 22nd Congress of the International Association for Caribbean Archaeology, July 24–30, 2005.

Mannur, Anita. *Culinary Fictions: Food in South Asian Diasporic Culture*. Philadelphia, PA: Temple University Press, 2010.

Mansingh, Laxmi and Ajai Mansingh. *Home Away from Home: 150 Years of Indian Presence in Jamaica, 1845–1995*. Kingston, Jamaica: Ian Randle Publishers, 1999.

Mehta, Ved. "Naturalized Citizen No. 984–4165," in *A Ved Mehta Reader: The Craft of the Essay*. New Haven, CT: Yale University Press, 1998, pp. 281–302.

Mehta, Venu Vrundavan. "An Ethnographic Study of Sectarian Negotiations among Diaspora Jains in the USA," MA thesis, Florida International University. 2017.

Melwani, Lavina. "What Are Over 200,000 Guyanese Hindus Doing in New York State? Far from their Grandfather's India, a Determined Community," *Hinduism Today*, August 5, 1995.

Melwani, Lavina. "Dazzling Success: Indians Have Displaced Jews for the Diamond Crown of the World," *Little India*, July, 2003.

Michael, Ali. *Raising Race Questions: Whiteness and Inquiry in Education*. New York: Teachers College Press, 2015.

Miller, Webb, and Roy W. Howard. *I Found No Peace: The Journal of a Foreign Correspondent*. New York: Literary Guild, 1936.

Mishra, Sangay K. *Desis Divided: The Political Lives of South Asian Americans*. Minneapolis, MN: University of Minnesota Press, 2016.

Mitter, Partha. *Much Maligned Monsters: A History of European Reactions to Indian Art*. New Delhi: Oxford University Press, 2013.

Mody, Susan L. *Cultural Identity in Kindergarten: A Study of Asian Indian Children in New Jersey*. London: Routledge, 2013.

Mohkamsing, Narinder. "Hinduism in Surinam," in Arvind Sharma (Ed.), *Encyclopedia of Indian Religions*. New York: Springer (forthcoming).

Moore, Adrienne. *Rammohun Roy and America*. Calcutta: Satis Chandra Chakravarti, 1942.

Morgan, Edmund S. "Columbus' Confusion About the New World," *Smithsonian Magazine*, 2009.

Morgan, Emily, Anna Stukenberg, and Andrew Tolliver. "The Immigration of Indian Food," *Future Tense EJournal*, August, 2011.

Mukherjee, Bharati. "Two Ways to Belong in America," *New York Times*, September 22, 1996.

Munshi, Kaivan. "From Farming to International Business: The Social Auspices of Entrepreneurship in a Growing Economy," NBER Working Paper No. 13065. April 2007.

Nair, Vineetha. "Santhigram: A Trailblazer of Ayurveda in America," *India Life and Times*, October 2017, pp. 45–47.

Narayan, Kirin. "Placing Lives Through Stories: Second-Generation South Asian Americans," in Diane P. Mines and Sarah Lamb (Eds.), *Everyday Life in South Asia*. Bloomington, IN: Indiana University Press, 2002.

Narayan, R. K. "My America," *Frontline*, October, 1985.

Narayanan, Vasudha. "Hinduism in Pittsburgh: Creating the South Indian 'Hindu' Experience in the United States," in John Hawley and Vasudha Narayanan (Eds.), *Life of Hinduism*. Berkeley, CA: University of California Press, 2007, pp. 231–248.

Neuman, Daniel M. "The Ecology of Indian Music in North America," *Bansuri* 1, 1984.

Neuman, Daniel M. "An Ethnography of the American Experience of Indian Music," in Louis A. Jacob (Ed.), *American Understanding of India*, papers read at a symposium at the Library of Congress, October 23–25, 1986. Washington, DC: Library of Congress, 2001.

New York Times. "Nasli M. Heeramaneck Dead: Dealer in Asian Art Objects," March 30, 1971.

Niebuhr, Reinhold. *Moral Man and Immoral Society: A Study in Ethics and Politics*. Louisville, KY: Westminster John Knox Press, 1932.

Okihiro, Gary Y. *The Columbia Guide to Asian American History*. New York: Columbia University Press, 2001.

142   Bibliography

Patel, Eboo. *Out of Many Faiths: Religious Diversity and the American Promise.* Princeton, NJ: Princeton University Press, 2018.

Patel, Manish V., *et al.*, "A Complex Multiherbal Regimen Based on Ayurveda Medicine for the Management of Hepatic Cirrhosis Complicated by Ascites: Non-randomized, Uncontrolled, Single Group, Open-Label Observational Clinical Study," *Evidence-Based Complementary and Alternative Medicine* 68 (2015): 8.

Prashad, Vijay. *The Karma of Brown Folk.* Minneapolis, MN: University of Minnesota Press, 2000.

Prashad, Vijay. *Uncle Swami: South Asian in America Today.* New York: The New Press, 2014.

Prothero, Stephen R. *A Nation of Religions: The Politics of Pluralism in Multireligious America.* Chapel Hill, NC: University of North Carolina Press, 2006.

Raeder, Samantha. "Thoreau's Biophilia: The Influence of Hindu Scriptures on Walden's Portrayal of Nature and the Divine," BA Honors thesis, University of Michigan, 2017.

Raj, Selva J. "Ammachi, the Mother of Compassion," in Karen Pechilis (Ed.), *The Graceful Guru: Hindu Female Gurus in India and the United States.* New York: Oxford University Press, 2004.

Ramaswamy, Krishnan, Nicolás A. T. De, and Aditi Banerjee. *Invading the Sacred: An Analysis of Hinduism Studies in America.* New Delhi: Rupa & Co, 2007.

Ramsoedh, Hans and Lucie Bloemberg. "The Institutionalization of Hinduism in Suriname and Guyana," in T. S. Rukmani (Ed.), *Hindu Diaspora: Global Perspectives.* New Delhi: Munshiram Manoharlal, 2001, pp. 123–164.

Rao, Ramesh. "It's India, Not South Asia," *The Cosmopolitan* 1(1) (2003): 27–39.

Reddy, Sita. "Asian Medicine in America: The Ayurvedic Case," *American Academy of Political and Social Science* 583(97) (2002): 97–121.

Rubin, Eric S. "America, Britain, and Swaraj: Anglo-American Relations and Indian Independence, 1939–1945," *India Review* 10(1) (2011): 40–80.

Ruckert, George. *Music in North India: Experiencing Music, Expressing Culture.* New York: Oxford University Press, 2004, p. 17.

Rudolph, Lloyd I. "Gandhi in the Mind of America," *Economic and Political Weekly* 45(47) (2010): 23–26.

Ruhomon, Peter. *Centenary History of the East Indians in British Guiana: 1838–1938.* Georgetown, Guyana: East Indians 150th Anniversary Committee, 1988, [1947].

Saks, Mike. "Plural Medicine and East-West Dialogue," in Dagmar Wujastyk and Frederick M. Smith (Eds.), *Modern and Global Ayurveda: Pluralism and Paradigms.* Albany, NY: State University of New York Press, 2008, pp. 29–41.

Saywell, Jr., R. M., Studnicki, J., Bean, J. A. and Ludke, R. L. "A Performance Comparison: USMG-FMG Attending Physicians," *American Journal of Public Health* 69(1) (1979): 57–62.

Sehgal, Deep. *Coolies: How Britain Re-Invented Slavery.* London: BBC, 2002.

Shah, Bindi. "Religion, Ethnicity and Citizenship: The Role of Jain Institutions in the Social Incorporation of Young Jains in Britain and USA," *Journal of Contemporary Religion* 32(2) (2017a): 299–314.

Shah, Dilip V. *Chitrabhanu: The Man of the Millennium.* Dallas, TX: independent, 2017b.

Shah, Natubhai. *Jainism: The World of Conquerors.* Delhi: Motilal Banarsidass Publishers, 2004.

Sharma, Arvind. *Gandhi: A Spiritual Biography.* New Haven, CT: Yale University Press, 2013.

Sharma, Brijendra Nath. "Jain Statues in American Museums and Private Collections," *Rajendra Jyoti* (1976): 131–133.

Sims, Alexander. "India Has the Largest Diaspora Population in the World, Says UN Report," *Independent*, January 14, 2016.

Slate, Nico. *Lord Cornwallis Is Dead: The Struggle for Democracy in the United States and India*. Cambridge, MA: Harvard University Press, 2019.

Slawek, Stephen M. "Ravi Shankar as Mediator between a Traditional Music and Modernity," in Stephen Blum, Philip V. Bohlman, and Daniel M. Neuman (Eds.), *Ethnomusicology and Modern Music History*. Urbana, IL: University of Illinois Press, 1993.

Srinivas, Tulasi. "'As Mother Made It': The Cosmopolitan Indian Family, 'Authentic' Food and the Construction of Cultural Utopia," *International Journal of Sociology of the Family*, January 1, 2006.

Subramaniam, Lakshmi. "Culture and Consumption: Classical Music in Contemporary India and the Diaspora," *Transforming Cultures eJournal* 3(1) (2008).

Svoboda, Robert. "The Ayurvedic Diaspora: A Personal Account," in Dagmar Wujastyk and Frederick M. Smith (Eds.), *Modern and Global Ayurveda: Pluralism and Paradigms*. Albany, NY: State University of New York Press, 2008, pp. 117–128.

The Economist "China Beat Columbus to It, Perhaps," January 12, 2006.

Thomas, Wendell Marshall. *Hinduism Invades America*. New York: Beacon Press, 1930.

Tudor, William. "Theology of the Hindoos, as Taught by Ram Mohun Roy," *The North-American Review and Miscellaneous Journal* 6(18) (1818): 386–393.

Tumbe, Chinmay. *India Moving: A History of Migration*. New Delhi: Penguin Random House, 2018.

Tuminello, Joseph A., III. "The Food-Drug Relationship in Health and Medicine," PhD dissertation, University of North Texas, 2018.

Twain, Mark. *Following the Equator: A Journey Around the World*. New York: Harper & Bros, 1929.

Urban, Hugh B. *Zorba the Buddha: Sex, Spirituality, and Capitalism in the Global Osho Movement*. Berkeley, CA: University of California Press, 2016.

Vallely, Anne. "From Liberation to Ecology: Ethical Discourses among Orthodox and Diaspora Jains," in Christopher Key Chapple (Ed.), *Jainism and Ecology*. Delhi: Motilal Banarsidass, 2000, pp. 193–216.

van der Veer, Peter and Steven Vertovec. "Brahamanism Abroad: On Caribbean Hinduism as an Ethnic Religion," *Ethnology* 30(2) (1991).

Varma, Roli. "High-Tech Coolies: Asian Immigrants in the US Science and Engineering Workforce," *iScience as Culture* 11(3) (2002): 337–362.

Varma, Roli. *Harbingers of Global Change: India's Techno-Immigrants in the United States*. Lanham, MD: Lexington Books, 2006.

Wade, Bonnie. "Indian Classical Music in North America: Cultural Give and Take," *Contributions to Asian Studies* 12 (1978).

Warikoo, Natasha K. *Balancing Acts: Youth Culture in the Global City*. Berkeley, CA: University of California Press, 2011.

Warrier, Maya. "Modern Ayurveda in Transnational Context," *Religion Compass* 5(3) (2011): 80–93.

Welch, Claudia. "An Overview of the Education and Practice of Global Ayurveda," in Dagmar Wujastyk and Frederick M. Smith (Eds.), *Modern and Global Ayurveda:*

Pluralism and Paradigms. Albany, NY: State University of New York Press, 2008, pp. 129–138.

Wujastyk, Dagmar and Frederick M. Smith. *Modern and Global Ayurveda: Pluralism and Paradigms.* Albany, NY: State University of New York Press, 2008.

Zia, Helen. *Asian American Dreams: The Emergence of an American People.* New York: Farrar, Strauss, and Giroux, 2001.

Index

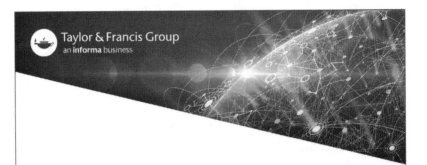